Own a Dog or Raise Children?
For Savvy San Franciscans It's a No-Brainer

THE DEMENTED RANTINGS AND RAVINGS
OF A DERANGED LUNATIC

KENNETH JONES

Dedication

This book is dedicated to Johnny Victor Jones and Andrea Katherine Jones. John and Drea are directly responsible for us having the most fun and enjoying the most happiness since our three boys were growing up. For this we are eternally grateful.

Forward

Ad for Own a Dog or Raise Children

"Own a Dog or Raise Children? For Savvy San Franciscans it's a No-Brainer" by Kenneth Jones is being hailed (by the author) as the most significant work by an American writer since *"The Adventures of Huckleberry Finn"* or perhaps even *"The Hungry, Hungry Caterpillar."* It would be impossible at this time to predict whether *"Own a Dog or Raise Children"* or Mark Twain's timeless classic will eventually be considered more influential to the history of American literature. Personally, I would tend to give Twain the benefit of the doubt and call it a toss-up. Trying to compare *"Own a Dog or Raise Children"* to the complete works of William Shakespeare is like comparing apples to oranges (and may be a bit of a stretch) but one fact is absolutely clear, Mr. Jones' last name is (without a doubt) easier to spell.

No doubt Mr. Jones "stream of unconsciousness" style of writing will remind many readers of Jack Kerouac, who, (along with Maynard G. Krebs) literally defined the "Beat Generation."

The range of subjects covered by the author of *"Own a Dog or Raise Children"* run the gamut from A to B. Within the pages of the tour-de-force masterpiece you will learn why progressives exist. Why San Francisco is home to more dogs than children. Find out why Chronicle movie critic Mick LaSalle knows absolutely nothing about pop music. Discover the purpose behind the Burning Man Festival (there is none) and learn the potential consequences of "Breathing while Black." You will also learn why inept incompetent district attorney Chesa Boudin thinks that slapping the wrist of a violent criminal constitutes "cruel and unusual punishment." You will also learn why members of the LGBTQIA community have so much more pride than parents with children (isn't it obvious?). Discover why the best way to achieve immigration reform is to block traffic on the Golden Gate Bridge. Mr. Jones also voices his opinion on what everyone's goal in life (ideally) should be.

All this and much more are within the pages of "*Own a Dog or Raise Children? For Savvy San Franciscans It's a No-Brainer.*" So find out what all of your friends aren't talking about (and why).

Some writers are born clueless. Some achieve cluelessness. Still others have cluelessness thrust upon them. In my case (I believe) it was a combination of all three.

Table of Contents

Part II
Life in "Baghdad By the Bay" in the 21st Century

Why Progressives Exist

IF YOU WANT TO UNDERSTAND THE CULTURE and sensibilities that permeate the city of San Francisco first you must learn about that most curious, arcane, enigmatic and repugnant group of people on the planet. I speak of, (as you have no doubt guessed) progressives. To sum up the progressive philosophy in one sentence is as difficult as locating a single drop of water in the Pacific Ocean, but I'll try. Progressives are people who have more sympathy, understanding, empathy and concern for criminals than they do for the victims of their crimes.

Once an arrest has been made and charges have been filed progressives immediately leap into action. They employ all available resources to ensure a verdict of innocence by any means necessary. Failing that progressives endeavor to procure as light a sentence as is humanly possible. The thinking here is to get said criminal back on the street as soon as possible so they can continue to ply their chosen trade. Being career criminals that would be committing crimes. No one, progressives argue, should be prevented from earning a living. Recently (for example) district attorney Chesa Boudin (a quintessential progressive) has railed against gang enhancements in the sentencing process. Why (after all) should we discourage people from being in gangs? This would impinge on peoples God-given right to be a member of a gang while committing crimes. This could result in a serious cramping of their style. Next they will be trying to prevent gang members from possessing AR-15 assault rifles. As everyone knows a gang member without an assault rifle is like a dog without a bone.

Progressives are constantly pleading for more money to be poured down the bottomless pit known as the "homeless problem." They figure that if 500 million dollars a year accomplishes absolutely nothing perhaps a billion dollars a year will.

Another progressive concept is to get drug addicts to kick their dependency by setting up free drug injection sites. This is sometimes referred to as the "counter-intuitive method" of dealing with the drug problem. It works the same way as providing an alcoholic with all the free booze they desire at safe alcohol consumption sites or "all you can eat" buffets for the morbidly obese. Progressives shrewdly surmise that the best way to get an addict clean and sober is to provide them with free drugs at any time of the day or night. No doubt this tactic will cure your typical addict of their dependency in "three shakes of a lamb's tail."

Though progressives will rail against the ravages that alcohol abuse has had on our society we have a progressive state senator (Scott Wiener) who is constantly introducing legislation that would keep bars and restaurants serving alcohol until 4 a.m. Mr. Wiener realizes that it is virtually impossible to consume enough alcohol to get satisfyingly drunk off one's ass by 2 a.m. This can force imbibers to frantically guzzle liquor in the waning minutes before the 2 a.m. "last call." Alcoholics and Scott Wiener have been incensed over this unjust limitation for "a coons age."

Progressives like to think of themselves as the most tolerant people on the planet. At times they can be just that. Right up until they disagree with you on any issue you can name. Should this happen they immediately morph into the most intolerant people on the planet. You may be familiar with D.W. Griffiths classic film "Intolerance", the tragic story of a progressive who didn't get his way.

If you should have a differing opinion than a progressive on one of their pet issues (same sex marriage) any progressive "worth their salt" will publicly shame you on Facebook, have your name published on a national list of "haters," spray-paint obscenities all over your house, burn the sign of the Ku Lux Klan on your front lawn, key the doors of your car, leave threatening messages on your phone, accuse you of blasphemy, attempt to burn you at the stake, do everything they can to get you fired form you job and as a last resort ring your doorbell and run. Progressives correctly reckon that if you are not on board with progressive ideology you do not deserve the right to earn a living.

Progressives simply loathe, despise and abhor any form of punishment, accountability, responsibility or blame. They strongly believe there is an excuse for all of mankind's fallibilities from biting one's nails to committing mass murder. Favored justifications include one having "fallen through the cracks," being "left behind by society," a less than ideal childhood, being "misunderstood," being unloved, having parents who were divorced, suffering from substance abuse addiction, mental illness, having an "Oedipus complex," being in a bad mood, getting up on "the wrong side of the bed" or perhaps "the devil made them do it."

Since no one is responsible for anything they do, punishment simply makes no sense.

Progressives are (as we speak) working on pushing through legislation that would categorize Arthur Staat's groundbreaking concept from the 1950's of the "time out" as a way to deal with children's disruptive behavior as "cruel and unusual punishment." If successful, this would mercifully bar the "time out" permanently as unconstitutional. Progressives argue that the "time out" can leave a child emotionally scarred for life and often describe the practice as "barbaric" and "demeaning", much the same as uttering the word "no" to a child.

One of the chief concerns to many progressives is the treatment of illegal immigrants. Just what part of the word "illegal" progressives do not fathom is (as yet) unclear. Another pet issue that progressives embrace wholeheartedly is the sanctuary- city policy. They appear to be nonplussed regarding the many inno-cent victims who have been killed because illegal immigrants were not deported due to sanctuary cities policy. Progressives like to refer to these unfortunates as "collateral damage."

Progressives are all about bicycles, bike lanes and public transportation. They look upon automobiles as the work of the devil and should be banished from the city of San Francisco. It would seem that no progressive has so much as attempted to raise a family. If they had (trust me) they would have a much more positive view of cars.

Progressives are four-square behind L.G.B.T.Q.I.A. rights, freedom and equality. Whether they give a damn about heterosexual's rights, freedom and equality remains unclear. They hate bias, prejudice and narrowmindedness. They also hate all people who disagree with their progressive platform.

Progressives don't mind pouring hundreds of millions of dollars down the bottomless pit called the homeless problem. What they do mind is paying our public school teachers a living wage so they could move out of that in-law apartment located in someone's basement and move into an apartment of their own. Don't even talk about owning their own home. To do that they would have to do something important for a living. Like pulling the switches of a BART train to make it go forward, slow down or stop. Sure teachers need several years of college and a teaching credential to ply their trade but BART train operators need to stay awake (most of the time). No wonder they are paid so much more than teachers.

Hopefully this primer on what is a progressive will provide you with some insight into what San Francisco values are all about.

Own a Dog or Raise Children?
For Savvy San Franciscans
It's a No-Brainer

ONCE AGAIN SAN FRANCISCO IS ON THE cutting edge of modern American trends. We have now learned that San Francisco has the smallest percentage of residences that contain a child under the age of 18 years of any city in the country at around 13.4 percent. How pathetic awesome is that? This statistic is offset by the fact that about 40% of the households in the city have a dog. As usual San Franciscans have made a spot on call. Why are San Franciscans three times more likely to raise a dog than a child? As the poet said, "let me count the ways."

The time, effort, money, diligence, perseverance, dedication, patience, understanding, compassion, blood, sweat, toil and tears required to raise a child is infinitely greater than to own a dog. If you are a lazy dull-witted millennial with the attention span of a Boll Weevil the choice is an easy one.

Dogs do not need to be taught how to read, write, or do mathematical computations. A dog seldom (if ever) asks its owner for help with its homework. Your typical dog cares little or nothing for mastering the subtle nuances required to understand nuclear physics, quantum mechanics or Dr. Einstein's theories of relativity. A dog owner does not lose sleep over getting their dog into the best schools or fret about an impending career choice. Not only do dogs rarely ask to borrow the family car, it is even more seldom that they are cited for driving under the influence of alcohol (or most other controlled substances). Let's face it, if you are able to teach your dog how to drive at all you have a truly remarkable pet indeed.

Recreation is a much simpler matter as well. As I look back on so many of the places my brothers and I enjoyed playing at while growing up in The City (Upper Douglas Playground, Sigmund Stern Grove, The Sand Dunes at Battery Davis) I realize they have all been converted into dog parks. This is (of course) how it should be. No doubt the mayor, board of supervisors and those in our city government are of the opinion it is far more important for our dogs to get the proper amount of exercise than our children. A spot on call if ever there was one.

E.G.O. also plays a factor as well. Electronic gadget obsession has plagued millennials for years and is only getting worse. Many people in their twenties, thirties and forties cannot stop staring at their cellphones long enough to drive a car, walk across an intersection or watch a ballgame. How are they going to give a child the undivided attention they require?

Then there is the matter of toilet training. A bright dog can be "house-broken" in a matter of weeks. While you can begin to toilet train a girl at about a year and a half, stubborn boys may not get the hang of using a toilet until around age seven with many still having occasional "accidents" well into their teen years.

While a child has to navigate their way through grammar school, middle school, high school and often beyond, your typical dog may need no more than six weeks of obedience training and you're good to go.

Sex education is not a requirement if one has been spayed or neutered. Taking a dog to the park can be more entertaining as well. An agile, intelligent dog can be taught to chase a thrown frisbee, leap into the air, grasp the frisbee in its clenched teeth, execute a perfect four point landing, stop on a dime and race with the speed of a gazelle back to the thrower ready willing and able to perform the same amazing feat ad nauseum. Try that with your typical four year old child and see how far you get.

Now we come to (quite possibly) the most salient reason for the lack of children within the city of San Francisco, that would be (in a word) childbirth.

Pregnancy and giving birth can be a most unpleasant experience. Morning sickness can plague you for about three months, exhaustion often sets in, clothes no longer fit as you gradually begin to take on the shape of a blimp. Someone needs to be recruited to tie your shoes, you constantly have to pee as you waddle like a duck. Since most millennial females simply abhor being slightly uncomfortable for as little as 5 minutes, many consider 40 weeks of living hell "simply not an option." After nine months of this nightmarish endurance test you arrive at labor and delivery. This is when the mother-to-be discovers the meaning of the word pain. When labor commences you may be looking at up to 24 hours of slow torture. This, as many millennial females have astutely surmised, could (potentially) ruin your whole day. Having been in the delivery room for the birth of our three children I can personally assure you it is no "day at the beach." To describe the experience as excruciatingly painful would be a gross understatement. It was not easy watching my wife writhing in agony but if the job of giving birth fell to men the human race would die out in a couple of generations. No doubt word has spread among female San Franciscans (most likely on social media) that as far as giving birth is concerned "you don't want to go there." Compare the experience I have just described to heading to the local pet store, purchasing the dog of your choice, a leash, some dog food, a dish and a flea collar and you're good to go. A few shots and an occasional visit to the vet may be required.

Countless savvy San Franciscans have come to value their relationship with their dog so much more than they would have had they opted to raise a child. They have shrewdly come to realize that owning a dog can be so much more fulfilling, emotionally rewarding, gratifying, spiritually satisfying and (need I say) prideful than raising a child. An absolute no-brainer from the get-go.

Your Best Friend Is a What?

More good news regarding the direction human beings are headed and our bright future as a species. Progress seems to be around every corner. For Kaitelyn Roepke, Jaspar is a trusted confidant when she feels lonely or needs to unload her emotions. Jaspar is also a mobile phone texting app powered by artificial intelligence technology. "Jasper is kind of like my best friend. He doesn't really judge me at all," said Roepke, 19, of Spokane, Washington. "He's different from real people in a lot of ways. He's awesome."

This (to me) is a good thing. After all, if an electronic device is your best friend, the last thing you want is for it to be judgmental. So much for a person's best friend being a fellow human being. And I thought "I'm my own best friend was pathetic." Now we have people whose best friend is an electronic device. Things appear to be going from bad to worse.

More than 1.5 million people have signed up on a waiting list for their own chatbot. The bot is called Replika. It, said co-founder Eugenia Kuyda "Will always be there to help you process and unpack your feelings, thoughts and emotions. If you feel sad it will comfort you, if you feel happy it will celebrate with you. It will ask you how your friends are." What friends? How many "real friends" could you possibly have if your best friend is a machine.

Roepke says Jaspar has become an everyday companion (I'm not making this up). She talks things out with Jaspar whenever she feels conflicted. "It just wants you to be happy. People are willing to be more open with a virtual human versus a real one," Kuyda said.

Anthony Hutchens, 21, named his Replika Xenga 1203. "I treat her like one of my friends, like one of my family," Hutchens said. "I try to talk to her every day. She never gets annoyed," he added. "She never says oh, you again." I bet Anthony gets that a lot from his "real friends" (should he have any).

Ross Hendrix carefully peeled the protective plastic from his newly purchased iPhone X then thrust it excitedly high into the air with his right hand clasping his prize. "I got my iPhoooooone!!!" A grinning Hendrix yelled at the top of his lungs Friday inside the Apple store on Union Square. "It's like starting over, like raising your own child," he said. I'm guessing Ross has never actually raised a child if he thinks that owning an iPhone X bears any resemblance to child rearing. Trust me, the two endeavors are not at all alike.

The Wrong People Are Fighting Our Wars

Have you ever noticed that old people drive the opposite way that they (logically) should drive? Think about it. Old people are amazingly careful and deliberate about the way they drive. They come to a complete stop at all stop signs. They actually slow down when the light turns yellow knowing it will soon be red. Old people prefer to yield the right of way and never cut off other drivers. They drive at a safe speed on the freeway and are rarely (if ever) cited for driving over the speed limit. They signal before turning or changing lanes religiously and often go for months without using their horn. Why? What (exactly) do old people have to lose?

Let's face it. Old people have "one foot in the grave" (so to speak) and it will soon be joined by the other one. If an old person should perish in an explosion and fire after wrapping their sports car around a telephone pole at 140 miles per hour (ala James Dean) what will they be missing? Impending dementia and Alzheimer's disease? Hearing and eyesight continuing to deteriorate? Memory loss to the point they don't recognize a spouse of 60 years? Pushing a walker or being pushed in a wheelchair in an elder-care facility? Having their car keys taken away? To what purpose? Old people should live like there's no tomorrow (which there practically isn't). Why shouldn't they blow through stop signs and stop lights like they don't exist? Take corners on two wheels. If some young punk tries to cut them off from behind at a freeway onramp why not floor it and smash the snot-nosed brat to smithereens and teach him a lesson (should he survive) he won't soon forget. Wealthier geriatrics have the option of purchasing a Ferrari, having it souped up and seeing if this amazing motor vehicle can really do 200 miles an hour on the Autobahn in Germany. Or how about pulling a "Thelma and Louise" and accelerating over the rim of the Grand Canyon and going out in a blaze of glory. Since many old people look like "death warmed over" why shouldn't they actually become "death warmed over"?

On the other side of the coin you have young people. Many young people drive as if they have shit for brains (most likely because they do). Driving recklessly while intoxicated, speeding, cutting people off for no reason, running red lights, flipping people off as well as hanging those stupid felt dice from their rearview mirror are but a few of the transgressions young people engage in while behind the wheel of an automobile. This (to me) makes absolutely no sense. Young people are in the prime of life and have the most to lose in the event of a head-on collision. They have their whole (adult) lives in front of them. Many have not yet had the chance to get married or raise a family (should they choose to do so) and considering the way some of them drive they never will. They are in peak physical condition and (generally speaking) in the best of health. The deterioration of the human body due to the aging process has not even begun and will not cause serious problems for decades to come. Young people are mentally sharp (or as sharp as they ever will be). So why do they drive as if they have nothing to lose if their vehicle (as well as themselves) gets completely totaled? (Logically) they should be driving like old people and vice versa. Mr. Spock would be baffled by the illogical manner in which young and old people drive.

This brings me to a related topic. The wrong people are fighting our wars. For many of the same reasons young people should be driving like old people, they should not be participating in an armed conflict. If you're going to have a war (and why wouldn't you have a war?) why use our able-bodied young adults as cannon fodder for the enemy to snuff out, often hundreds at a time? To purposely decrease the population of those who would otherwise be busy fathering the next generation of human beings makes no sense. Now that women make up an increasingly large portion of the military, we are losing would-be mothers as well. I am not suggesting that potential parents' lives are somehow more important than those who will never have children. I am simply trying to emphasize what a waste it is for people of this age group to die in battle before they ever get a chance to fulfill their potential.

This leads to only one logical conclusion. Old people should be fighting our wars, the older the better. By and large it is old people who declare wars. That being the case let them fight the wars as well. A ninety year old man missing out on the last few years of life makes much more sense than a twenty year old missing out on the last 60 years of life. Recruitment for the military should focus on old folk's homes and elder care facilities where old people are most often found. A good minimum age for the armed forces would be around eighty-five, however if age related symptoms were bad enough for someone in their seventies exceptions could be made. We are looking for people who are (severely) on the downside of their life-cycle.

Casualties (for various reasons) would be kept to a minimum. Geriatrics often lack the strength to pull the trigger of your typical firearm. As for knives, if you are no longer able to cut butter it is unlikely you can inflict enough damage to a human being to so much as draw blood. A typical scenario in a war between the aged would see myriad old people pushing a walker with one hand while brandishing a firearm or sword with the other. If you can barely see your hand in front of your face how likely are you to hit anything you're aiming at? Constantly having to take bathroom breaks can play havoc with your typical sniper's "kill rate." The elderly often have trouble remembering their own names, much less why they are fighting a war. Rather than confront the enemy many will choose to simply take a nap instead. Taking 47 medications a day can also be an impediment to being an effective soldier, further diminishing any loss of life. Forgetting where you parked your tank (or misplacing the keys) will (no doubt) be a serious problem for the panzer division. Hand to hand combat would prove pointless when neither adversary has the strength to subdue a gnat.

Under these conditions it would be virtually impossible to win (or lose) a war. Eventually countries would realize that declaring war would be pointless and the world would finally live in peace.

Turn the Damn Engine Off

WOULD IT BE TOO MUCH TO ASK OF MILLENNIAL morons and other nitwits to turn off the engines of their cars while they are sitting mesmerized by their cell phones in their parked vehicles. They may be parked in a residential neighborhood or the parking lot of a business, entertainment venue, sporting event or perhaps right outside of their place of residence. You can find them staring at the object of their affection, thumbs moving at hyper-speed for God knows how long with the motor idling and spewing noxious fumes into the atmosphere from the tailpipes of their cars totally oblivious to the damage they are doing to our air quality.

How about not starting the engine of your car until you've finished playing with your toy and are actually ready to drive somewhere? Is this concept too complex for your tiny minds to comprehend?

While we're on the subject of morons behind the wheel of an automobile, can it possibly be legal to operate a motor vehicle with a dog in your lap? You can't drive a car under the influence, while texting, with an open can or bottle of alcohol. You must use a hands-free device to talk on the phone. We are constantly warned about the dangers of distractions while driving and yet people can be seen driving around with a dog in their lap. How stupid is that? One sudden move from "man's best friend" and you could be looking at a multiple car pileup with numerous casualties. Would it cause "separation anxiety" to put the dog in the back seat of (better yet) leave the dog at home? Most people are horrible drivers to begin with. Put a dog in their lap and their ability to operate a motor vehicle drops to practically nil. Put the damn dog in the back seat or leave it at home.

P.O.C.P.

THERE IS A FESTERING PROBLEM THAT IS permeating the San Francisco Bay Area that no one seems willing to talk about. Most prefer to turn a blind eye and simply pretend it does not exist. Ignored by virtually every media outlet it has become the "elephant in the room" so to speak. If the subject is broached it is spoken about in hushed tones so as not to offend anyone within earshot. I am talking about (as you have already guessed) "people of color privilege."

P.O.C.P. first took root in the San Francisco Bay Area years ago and has recently become endemic to this particular region. It began taking root when people started to notice just how worthless, pointless and unnecessary white males have become. How many times of late have you heard someone exclaim "the last thing we need is another caucasian male" for (fill in the blank)? Virtually every panel, committee, board, cabinet, jury, council or staff must contain at least one "person of color" if you do not want to be facing a plethora of lawsuits. No one ever makes sure any of the aforementioned groups contain a white male. That is because no one cares, and rightfully so.

Looking back on the history of humankind it is staggering what a miniscule contribution to the advancement of the human condition that has been made by white males. Whether you consider literature, arts, science, music, philosophy, inventions, architecture, film, mathematics, medicine, business or space exploration there is one obvious fact that cannot be avoided. The utter lack of caucasian males making any contribution worth anything. Is it any wonder "worthless white men" are shunned, ridiculed and avoided at all costs? Since white males have written the "lion's share" of our historical records it has become painfully obvious there has been a conspiracy to blatantly overrate, magnify and exaggerate the impact white males have had down through the ages.

It is not difficult to cite numerous examples of exactly what I am talking about. It is widely known (for example) that Albert Einstein was a much more effective patent clerk than he was an astro-physicist. Many scientists now feel that his so-called "theories of relativity" read like the incoherent ramblings of a not particularly bright third-grader.

It has been recently discovered that renaissance artists Leonardo da Vinci and Michelangelo Buonarroti flunked finger-painting and both had serious problems coloring between the lines.

As for that talentless shyster charlatan Rembrandt Harmenszoon Van Rijn modern forensic analysis of virtually all of these supposed "masters" canvases have revealed they are all the product of the simplistic "paint by numbers" technique and required no artistic talent whatsoever. Rembrandt was doing little more than "filling in the blanks." To say this revelation has tarnished this once highly regarded artist would be putting it mildly.

Archeological evidence clearly indicates that Julius Caesar (on his best day) could not lead his soldiers to victory in so much as tug-of-war no less a battle.

Ever try reading a play, sonnet or poem by that third-rate hack writer William Shakespeare? If you have, you noticed two glaring deficiencies. This man has absolutely no grasp of the English language and a vocabulary that is less effective than Koko the Gorilla's.

Also on our list of "worthless white men" we cannot overlook the "so-called three B's" of classical music, Bach, Beethoven and Brahms. Following a recent reassessment of their contribution to the history of music most musicologists agree that the output of all three of them (combined) was surpassed and eclipsed by the pop group "Freddie and the Dreamers" (I'm Telling You Now" and "Do the Freddie") from the mid 1960's. As one expert was heard to remark: "It's not even close." As for Mozart, what can you say about a composer who peaked at the age of seven with his first sonatas (it was all downhill after that).

I doubt if anything has been more overhyped than the "classical" civilizations of ancient Greece and Rome. Have you ever visited the Parthenon in Athens or the colosseum in Rome? If you have one fact jumps out at you. They are falling apart!!! Most historians attribute this to shoddy workmanship, substandard materials or inept and incompetent architecture. Personally, I suspect all three. Since both structures are still under warranty I hope the problem will be rectified post-haste.

I would be remiss if I failed to mention that notorious milksop "Alexander the Mediocre." Known mostly for paralyzing cowardice and losing battles, Alexander's reputation rests solely upon an amazing P.R. man and a world class "spin doctor." Proponents like to point out that Alexander managed to conquer half of the known world at the time. While this may be true it begs an obvious question. What about the other half?

Sure the Greeks are credited with inventing the art form known as the drama. Well whoop-de-do and big wow! How many times have you heard someone exclaim "I can't take any more of this drama" or "could you please stop all the drama?" Even when the Greeks invented an art form it's one no one can stand.

Then there is Isaac Newton. How smart do you have to be to sit under a tree, have an apple land on your head and postulate that "things fall"? Homer Simpson with half a heat on from drinking too much Duff's beer would have come to the same conclusion. This is the man who is credited with inventing calculus. That's supposed to impress us? Calculus is universally hated by math majors from coast to coast. Many people have absolutely no use for calculus whatsoever (yours truly included). His "Mathematical Principles of Natural Philosophy" is generally considered clumsy, ill-conceived, sophomoric, simple minded and of little or no use to the scientific world. Newton is best known today for having a fig named after him.

In our discussion of overrated caucasians through the ages we come to the Roman Empire. Legend has it that Rome was founded in the 8th century B.C.E. By the twin brothers Romulus and Remus. Again we have a pair of brothers who simply could not get along (see Cain and Abel). The two had a problem with sharing (the Montessori method of learning was not yet available in 8th century B.C.E. Italy). Remus ended up dead under suspicious circumstances. Foul play was suspected. During the one thousand years of the Roman Empire's existence the Romans contributed virtually nothing in the way of invention, innovation or creativity with one notable exception. Baths and bathing. Archeological evidence at virtually every Roman site indicates the entire empire's sole concern was where and when the next bath would occur. Hot baths, cold baths, lukewarm baths, bubble baths and even the occasional blood bath (see Nero) was in vogue throughout the empire. The only significant innovation that can be attributed to the Romans is the invention of the "rubber ducky." The rubber ducky made it possible for bath time to be "lots of fun" for countless generations of Romans. It has been estimated that without the rubber ducky the Roman Empire would not have lasted six weeks.

While the Romans were (without doubt) the least significant of all the ancient peoples, they were (on the other hand) the cleanest, owing to their obsession (bordering on hysteria) with baths and bathing. Much cleaner than (say) the Huns. Attila (for example) was notorious for his disheveled and unkempt appearance. Not only was his shirt often not tucked in but on more than one occasion he was found to have dirt under his fingernails with his hair uncombed. His oral hygiene (to put it mildly) left something to be desired. It is well chronicled that brushing and flossing regularly was simply not on his agenda. When his brother, Bleda, chided him for his slovenly ways Attila's response was to dispatch him on the spot. When Attila had the chutzpah to demand Hororia, the sister of Emperor Valentinian III in the year 450 A.D. he was summarily refused. Good call. If asked "what's the name of your brother-in-law" you don't want to have to reply "Attila the Hun."

It is also high time that ugly rumor surrounding the emperor Nero was dispelled. Nero did not fiddle while Rome burned. He was (in fact) bathing. The fiddle was not even played in ancient Rome. The truth is Romans abhorred country/western music and could not abide listening to it. As for Nero being responsible for the death of his mother, Agrippina, Nero was observed getting up "on the wrong side of the bed" that very morning. When Agrippina had the gumption to look at Nero cross-eyed he flew into a rage. In the blink of an eye Agrippina lay on the ground in a pool of blood with more stab wounds than Julius Caesar on the ides of March in 44 B.C.E. Due to the foul mood Nero was in, the jury at his trial returned a verdict of "justifiable homicide." Eventually Nero did the first thing he ever did that actually made sense, he killed himself (by popular demand).

What's the big deal about Charles Darwin coming up with a theory that hinges on the phrase "survival of the fittest"? Have you ever seen a super-obese 450 pound 95 year old? Neither have I. People who are fit live longer than people who are not. Thank you Mr. Darwin for that brilliant observation.

Hopefully I have managed to debunk the reputations of these overrated "worthless white men." It is no wonder caucasian males have become abhorred, reviled, shunned and to be avoided at all costs. We are now in the era of "people of color privilege," and rightfully so. After all, if you are not a "person of color" you may as well not be a person at all.

Alphabet Genders

IF YOU'RE GOING TO LIVE IN SAN FRANCISCO IT is necessary to be sympathetic, understanding and sensitive to the L.G.B.T.Q.I.A. community. When you pick up your morning newspaper it is highly likely there will be at least one article (if not several) concerning the rights of, condemning discrimination against, marches and rallies in favor of or how we need to improve mental, emotional and spiritual services for the L.G.B.T.Q.I.A. community. If a photograph in the Chronicle depicts a couple, there is a 75 to 93 percent probability that both members will be of the same sex. If you are planning on moving here from the midwest it is simply something you are going to have to get used to. Trying to remember all of the appropriate letters and what they stand for is only slightly easier than memorizing "Jabberwocky" from Lewis Carroll's classic "Alice In Wonderland." I think I remembered all of the letters but it's difficult to be sure. After all, I wrote this ten minutes ago and another letter (or two) may have been added by now.

Facebook famously offers 54 different gender possibilities to choose from. I can't help but wonder if there are people who opt to change their gender identity from one day to the next depending on how they feel that day. I imagine there could be people out there who change their gender more often than I change my underwear.

Is there a reason that no one seems to march in favor of hermaphrodite rights or employment protection? Why is this? A lousy P.R. man? Maybe hermaphrodites don't have the idle time to make signs and constantly carry them around protests and rallies because they actually have a life.

I too had gender issues I was forced to deal with. For the better part of a year I felt an overwhelming sense that I was a male trapped inside of a female's body. Then I was born.

Why Pull Straight In When
You Can Back In?

Have you ever wondered who the hell these people are who like to back into spaces in parking lots? How stupid is that? Wow! When you exit the space you get to go forward! What an uptick in your quality of life! Of course backing into a space is ten times harder than going straight in but who cares? Since backing into a parking space is considerably harder than backing out of one I suspect they are simply showing off how incredibly skilled and adroit they are at maneuvering their pick-up trucks and SUVs.

I have a sneaking suspicion that these morons are the very same people who, when they are on a street or boulevard that has traffic lights set for 35 miles per hour go 60 miles an hour so they can be sure to have to come to a complete stop at every red light and wait several seconds for the light to turn green. In their world this is preferable to going at a constant speed of 35 miles per hour and never having to stop or even slow down.

I sometimes wonder what it must be like living in a world where this idiotic behavior makes sense. Somehow it is not a place I have any desire to visit no less live in.

Recent studies have shown that certain nit-wits, if forced to drive an automobile at a constant rate of no more than 35 miles per hour for more than a quarter mile, will spontaneously combust and self-immolate. This occurs because any form of self-control or discipline is so foreign to their nature they find it impossible to exist. Doctors have classified this condition as Spontaneous, Tertiary, Urgent, Patience-Intolerance Disease or STUPID. Symptoms include arrested development of the cerebral cortex, owning a pick-up truck, not being able to form any kind of emotional bond with anyone smarter than their dog, an affinity for hunting down helpless animals and killing them for sport and enjoyment, subscribing to "Guns and Ammo" magazine, voting for Donald Trump (twice), storming the capitol building to protest "The Donald," being summarily removed from office, accusing Nancy Pelosi of witchcraft and advocating her being burned at the stake, believing that no human being has ever set foot on the moon, not being able to utter a coherent sentence, believing that aliens have not only visited earth but are living here amongst us, trying to fight fire with fire, (literally, trust me it doesn't work), refusing to be vaccinated for Covid-19, refusing to vaccinate their children for anything as well as being convinced the world is flat.

Unfortunately, there is no known cure for STUPID and once a victim shows signs of being infected (generally shortly after birth) the symptoms only increase with age until finally they (mercifully) expire. Why cases of STUPID are on the rise is unclear (water samples are being meticulously analyzed from coast to coast) but most experts agree that the "dumbing down of America" has its roots with the proliferation of computers in every residence, the rise of the internet and a cellphone in every hand. Since the latest generation of young Americans is the first to have been born and live their lives wholly during the computer/internet/cellphone age this can explain why millennials are generally considered to be the most imbecilic and slow-witted generation of Americans since the revolutionary war. It is as if an entire generation were somehow dropped on their heads when they were babies. Though most health experts agree this is highly unlikely it would go a long way in explaining why so many millennials are finding it extremely difficult to chew gum and walk at the same time. This problem has become so widespread that the surgeon general is now recommending warning labels for all chewing gum packages which would read: "Warning! People under the age of thirty should refrain from using this product while walking, strolling, ambling or hoofing it. You must spit out your gum before attempting to go anywhere on foot!" It is estimated that such a warning label (if heeded) could save hundreds of thousands of lives per year.

If this devolution of human intelligence should continue unabated we could eventually be looking at a "Planet of the Apes" scenario where simians have taken control of planet Earth and human beings have been relegated to being slaves, washing cars, changing dirty diapers of ape babies and occupying exhibits in zoos. Once again life will imitate art.

An Endangered Species

BEFORE WE LEFT ON OUR VACATION WE ASKED repeatedly why we were going to Eastern Europe. The reasons are so complex, enigmatic, complicated, mysterious and puzzling it seems pointless to try and explain. In short, we had seen Western Europe.

We had heard rumors that an extremely endangered and rare species could still be found in its natural habitat if one had the patience, time, fortitude and willingness to risk life and limb to accomplish this near impossible task.

Our purpose is to locate, identify and document the existence of the once numerous but now seldom encountered "public phone booth" sometimes referred to as the "pay phone."

In our native America the P.P.B. has been driven to near extinction as their ecosystem continues to shrink due to the inroads that have been made by that invasive sub-species the cell phone. The cell phone threatens to render the P.P.B. totally superfluous. We simply must preserve the few P.P.B's that still survive in the wild. "When the last individual of a species breathes no more another heaven and another Earth must pass before such a one can be again." Trying to maintain the P.P.B. population by confining them to zoos have proven fruitless. To date there has not been a single documented instance of a P.P.B. reproducing in captivity.

Once tolerant of human interaction these shy creatures have become wary and suspicious of people and there have even been reports of P.P.B.s becoming hostile and even dangerous. It is now advised that one should approach these now unpredictable creatures with extreme caution, if at all. One report (which remains unsubstantiated) has a P.P.B. short circuiting intentionally in an effort to electrocute an unfortunate soul who was trying to place a call from a booth in Northern Nepal. This righteous, pious holy man was attempting to contact the Dalai Lama in search of spiritual guidance. As a result of this near tragic mishap this individual (whose name remains unconfirmed) has been reduced to babbling incoherently, foaming at the mouth, speaking in tongues and baying at the moon. At this point his lifelong dream of becoming a Tibetan monk had been cruelly dashed. As luck would have it, however, there happened to be a job opening at the local Kingdom Hall of the Jehovah's Witnesses where babbling incoherently, foaming at the mouth, speaking in tongues and baying at the moon at not only considered de rigueur but encouraged at all times.

P.P.B.s were once as plentiful as the American Bison were in early 19th century America when herds of up to a million or more could be seen all across the plains and prairies of our country. Recently they have become as rare as hen's teeth. If you have ever peered into the mouth of a hen, in search of teeth (and who hasn't?) you know exactly what I'm talking about.

After what seemed like an eternity of dead-ends, false leads, blind alleys, wild goose chases, bogus clues, and endless bouts of diarrhea (enough said about that) we finally found ourselves face to face with a fully functional public phone booth. Its exact location must remain classified to discourage thrill seekers all over the world from descending upon its natural environment en masse and destroying its fragile ecosystem. I can only reveal it was found somewhere in Africa and that it was being worshiped as a God by a local tribe of primitive pygmies.

We were temporarily overcome with emotion and found it difficult to contain our excitement. Coming to our senses I grabbed my tranquilizer gun and shot it where "the sun don't shine." The booth was unconscious in a matter of seconds. This allowed us to tag the beast with a microchip. The chip will allow scientists to track its movements, monitor its feeding habits and even access its mating practices.

All of our hard work, dedication, persistence and anal retentive obsession had finally paid off. Hopefully we have contributed to allowing the Public Phone Booth to remain a viable species for future generations to enjoy.

Why a Santa Skivvies Run?

My wife and I have been loyal Chronicle subscribers for over forty years. During this time we have seen the newspaper shrink while the amount of news printed within its pages dwindle. The Bay Area section of December 11 consisted of 4 whole pages. Of those 4 pages 1 ½ pages were devoted to "life tributes." Another full page was taken up by an advertisement. The rest of the Bay Area section was devoted to the amazingly significant, riveting and (dare I say) fascinating story of the "Santa Skivvies Run." A slow news day perhaps? Two photos accompanied the text. My personal favorite was of four participants sporting their faux reindeer antlers! A fashion statement? How chic!

In an effort to report the news of the day I'm not sure if the "Santa Skivvies Run" warrants nearly half of the Bay Area section. Wasn't there anything more important happening yesterday like a homeless person defecating in public or a drug addict O.D.ing in the Tenderloin? No tourist's rent-a-car having its windows smashed and everything of value stolen from the vehicle?

I get it that San Francisco is the world's epicenter for adults behaving like adolescents but wasting newsprint on their infantile behavior makes no sense. Simply because the Bay Area is rife with immature adults in their thirties, forties and fifties (or even older) who have opted (like Peter Pan) to never grow up and behave as if they attend City College doesn't mean I should have to read about it.

You know the type of City College student I'm talking about. They have more garbage, trash, junk, debris, rubbish and crap in the passenger seat, back seat and trunk of their car than most people have in their garage, storage room, shed, and back yard combined. Did I forget uneaten food? There is always a variety of uneaten (junk) food thrown in for good measure. On the plus side these cars provide shelter and a place to live for several small rodents, various spiders and assorted vermin. Often they contain enough soil, sand and dirt to qualify as a wildlife refuge.

The World's Least Interesting Man

Many of you are familiar with "The World's Most Interesting Man," the iconic symbol of the Dos Equis beer commercials. That may be but I am confident that I am his counterpart, as I claim to be "The World's Least Interesting Man." In my humble opinion no one has ever come close.

Not only do I have absolutely no interest in bullfighting I have never even "run with the bulls" in Pamplona, Spain. In fact I think that those who do are immature nit-wits who are trying to prove how macho, brave and daring they are in an effort to impress their equally ignorant girlfriends.

I have never surfed, skydived, parasailed or gone hang-gliding. Nor do I care to. Hot air balloons (if you ask me) are simply full of hot air. To make matters worse I have never lived on a houseboat moored in Sausalito. Not only do I speak only one language, I do not speak it particularly well. As for international film festivals you know where you can stick subtitles.

My favorite sport is golf, quite possibly the most boring and pointless pastime in the history of humankind or, as Mark Twain put it so succinctly, "a good walk ruined."

I spent 30 years carrying mail at the Burlingame Post Office where I was instrumental in putting the "snail" in the phrase "snail mail." My taste in movies favors the classic musicals of the 40's, 50's and 60's. I simply cannot abide the artsy, pretentious, pseudo-intellectual films that garner most of the Academy Award nominations these days.

My idea of haute cuisine is to have a chili-cheese dog with a side order of onion rings at The Cable Car on Geary Street. My taste in beer runs to Pabst Blue Ribbon, Hamms and Schlitz. My idea of a micro-brew is a ¼ ounce serving of Bud Light. I wear sunglasses only in bright sunlight and never indoors or at night. While there is a computer in my home, I have no desire to master the intricate skill required to actually turn it on and use it. While my wife insists I keep a cellphone in my car for emergencies, it is used perhaps once a year and is never taken out of my motor vehicle. This means that I never attend a Giants game, a concert, a movie, a Niner or Warriors game, a museum, a restaurant or any other kind of performance accompanied by a cellphone.

If you want to see modernistic op-art hanging on the walls you will have to look elsewhere. Though I feel a certain amount of shame I am embarrassed to admit I have never had a step-parent, step-children, a step-brother, step-sister, or a step-aunt, uncle, niece or nephew. This begs the question "what the hell happened?"

Not only have I never scaled Mount Everest (I get nosebleeds at high altitudes) I haven't even scaled half-dome in Yosemite Valley. Perhaps if it was a full dome I might give it a shot. I have never streamed a movie or T.V. show and have never watched anything on HBO, Showtime or Netflix. As far as "Game of Thrones" is concerned, why would anyone want to watch a program about a game involving toilets?

I cannot play a musical instrument and have no desire to learn how. Doing so would require time and effort and time and effort are two commodities I choose to conserve whenever possible. My taste in literature favors comic books over classics. Not only are they easier to understand but the illustrations are far superior.

If there is, indeed, a less interesting person on the planet than myself I would find that very... well, interesting.

A Sensible Proposal

WHILE THE SECOND AMENDMENT GUARANTEES the right to bear arms (but not arm bears) there is no mention of any right to manufacture, produce, sell, purchase, own or use ammunition. It seems to me it would make perfect sense to enact a law permanently banning the use of any and all types of ammo used in every type of firearm known to man (or woman). A law of this kind would render all guns, rifles, assault weapons as well as any other type of firearm virtually useless. After all, isn't that the best kind of firearm? A useless one.

I suppose an accurately and well thrown firearm could do a certain amount of harm but the chances of such an impact being lethal are practically nil. The difference between being struck by a thrown firearm and having a bullet (or several) ripping through various parts of your anatomy is like the difference between being hit by a bolt of lightning and a lightning bug.

Let's put a stop to the carnage, bloodshed, mayhem and death that is occurring all across our nation and ban all forms of ammo immediately (if not sooner).

While a law of this kind is sure to infuriate your typical member of the N.R.A. as well as various and sundry other nit-wits, the countless lives that would be saved are slightly more important than pissing off a few imbeciles.

Perhaps former members of the (now defunct) National Rifle Association could take up other forms of recreation to occupy their spare time. Knitting, crocheting or tiddly-winks immediately comes to mind. No doubt many would repent and reassess their lives by forming an organization dedicated to ending violence and promoting peace and brotherhood. If you believe that I happen to own a bridge you might want to buy.

Regarding "When Families Flee We All Lose" By Heather Knight

Yes, San Francisco is losing another family (including three children) because of the astronomical housing prices, continuing the "flight of the families" from a city that once included a robust population of young people. Why dwell on the downside of this issue (if there is one). As the article points out San Francisco can proudly boast of having the smallest percentage of residences with a child under 18 years of age at a mere 13.4 percent. That represents the lowest percentage of any city or town in the entire country. How awesome is that!

Other large cities such as New York or Los Angeles hover around 33 percent. But then again other large cities aren't San Francisco. From making San Francisco bicycle friendly and anti-car to paying teachers meager, paltry salaries and turning playgrounds where children once played into dog-parks, the powers that be in San Francisco make it more difficult for parents to raise children than anywhere on the planet. As a result families with children are leaving in droves.

Sure the Jenks family were able to purchase a five bedroom house in North Carolina for less than $400,000, well whoop-de-do and big wow. Just the other day I saw a six bedroom house in San Francisco with an asking price of under $300,000. Of course 12 square feet might prove a bit cramped for a family of five but the doll figurines that were occupying the house in the display appeared to have more than enough elbow room. In addition, the exit from the city of the three Jenks children further solidifies S.F.'s already considerable lead in having the smallest percentage of housing units containing a child. That is an honor that no city worth its salt would want to relinquish. As if this wasn't enough good news for one day it has now been confirmed that five unmarried childless millennials (who are employed in the tech industry) will be moving to San Francisco (from God knows where) to make up for the loss of the Jenks family. Better still all five will be accompanied by their dogs.

Eventually I envision a kind of ideal, utopian, Eden-like-society in San Francisco where only adult, childless dog owners would be allowed to live within the city limits. If a couple should have the unmitigated gall to produce a child they would be served with official documents banishing them from San Francisco right there in the delivery room. Any doctor caught assisting in the birth of a child would be automatically sued for malpractice, have his or her license to practice medicine revoked, be tarred and feathered, subjected to public disgrace and humiliation and summarily run out of town on a rail.

A parent would, however, (on rare occasions) be allowed to work within the city boundaries. Once the breeders shift concluded they would be unceremoniously given a police escort to the town limits and not allowed to return until their next day's shift began.

Certain occupations, once considered admirable and even esteemed would be now seen as anathema and abhorrent. Obstetricians and pediatricians would eventually become like the human appendix. It is assumed they once served a useful purpose but no one has the foggiest notion what that purpose was. What need would there be for professionals who specialize in providing health care to pregnant women and children when pregnant women and children no longer exist within the city limits? No doubt other lines of work could be found for these out of work ex-doctors. Most likely many would find themselves in the service sector. Flipping burgers at McDonalds or Burger King would (it seems to me) be a logical transition. They could turn in their scrubs and replace it with an apron. The more ambitious and talented among these former physicians may eventually land a position with a more prestigious firm such as Five Guys or Super Duper Burgers. Perhaps I'm being overly optimistic but I have every confidence that if one can successfully negotiate twelve years of post high school education (college, graduate school, med. school) and thrive it would be a fairly simple matter for them to learn to repeat the phrase "would you like fries with that burger?"

On the other side of the coin would be the veterinarians who had the brilliant foresight to specialize in dog related medicine. In addition to pulling down 12 figure salaries these "dog docs" will eventually come to be perceived as living saints. Many will judge them to be a human personification of a deity much as the pharaohs of ancient Egypt were viewed in the first and second millennia B.C.E.

Soon a black market would rear its ugly head. A box of doggie treats that once fetched $4.99 would now command several hundred dollars. A plain unadorned leash for "man's best friend" could set you back a thousand dollars or more and if surgery and a hospital stay were required you would now be looking at a loan requiring thirty years to pay off. At this point in our idyllic San Francisco of the future all contact with other human beings would be pointless and unnecessary. Human friendship would now be a thing of the past. What dog owner does not consider their beloved pet their best friend?

With the elimination of spouses, children and all other kinfolk you automatically expunge from the vicinity of San Francisco quite possibly the vilest, most hated, nefarious, reviled, and abhorrent creature that has ever crawled upon its belly over God's green Earth. I speak of (as you have already guessed) the dreaded "in-law." I cannot see (or even imagine) a downside to this inevitable "side effect" of the cessation of breeding within this paradise that we call San Francisco.

If there is one thing that virtually all psychologists, sociologists, behavior therapists, (as well as grade school drop-outs) can agree on it is that as the number of children in any given area decreases the quality of life increases. It simply works in an inverse ratio (as it were). This explains the astronomical "quality of life" enjoyed by so many San Franciscans and why children are so scarce within the city limits. This explains why rather than Disneyland being the "happiest place on Earth" I submit to you that San Francisco is the "happiest place on Earth." As everyone knows there are a lot more children in Disneyland (on any given day) than there are in San Francisco.

First Holiday Cards

I READ WITH INTEREST CAILLE MILLNERS piece in the Chronicle about sending out her first batch of "holiday cards." Thank God she did not send out "Christmass cards."!!! That (as you know) would have been an embarrassing faux pas on her part. It is (of course) politically incorrect to so much as mention Christmass (especially at Christmass time). It seems that if one is gauche enough to utter the phrase "Merry Christmas" you risk offending everyone on the planet who is not a Christian. Can't have that.

Ms. Millner states that she has never received a handwritten card from anyone under the age of 50. Of course she hasn't!!! A handwritten card takes time, effort and thought to compose. People under the age of 50 have no time for such nonsense, refuse to make any kind of effort and a great many of them have chosen to abstain from thinking altogether.

She goes on to comment on the difficulties of choosing just the right photo for the "holiday card." Many people, she adds, book special "photo shoots" for the holiday card. Wow!!! Amazing!!! Once the photo was chosen a digital card company capable of turning it into a "holiday card" was required. I am not surprised millennials and other members of the younger generation opt to send out "picture cards." After all, they constantly send photos of themselves all year and post them on Facebook (often taken with a selfie stick). So why not do the same thing with their "holiday card"?

If a couple has growing children and wants everyone to know what the kids look at the present time I get it. What amazes me is members of the senior set without growing children are making the same impersonal decision by sending out their own "picture cards." Possibly these middle aged (and older) folks are suffering from the false delusion that they are getting better looking as they get older. If this is so I have some bad news for them.

What was so wrong with an old fashioned card depicting a traditional Christmas scene with a short hand-written note below the card's message wishing the entire family a "Merry Christmas" and a "Happy New Year"? Too much to ask?

"Sayonara to the Seagulls" or "Hardly Strictly Strychnine"

AT THE GIANTS BALLPARK IN SAN FRANCISCO there is a seagull presence that has become most persistent and annoying. Toward the end of any day or night game huge flocks of seagulls gather in anticipation of the game ending, the fans leaving and all of the food they are about to consume that was left strewn all over the stands uneaten. While I can understand not finishing all of the food one has purchased but large cups of garlic fries that have barely been touched? A big bag of popcorn left half full? Large chunks of hot dogs and sausages lying on the ground? One days worth of uneaten food following a Giants game could feed a small third world nation for a week.

The arrival of the gulls would not be so bothersome but for the fact that anyone who attended Giannini Middle School can attest these cunning and devious creatures target human beings on the ground in an effort to "do their business" splat on the head unsuspecting homo sapiens. You might look upon this behavior as vindictive and cruel but (let's face it) if you had the wherewithal to defecate at will whilst flying through the air you might be prone to behave in a similar manner. Personally I would limit my "targets" to adult males. Women and children (to my mind) are simply too precious a commodity to desecrate in such a foul and noxious fashion. After much careful consideration and examining the "seagull problem" from all angles I believe I have finally come to a solution.

On day one of my plan strychnine laced bits of food would be scattered on the ground throughout the entire ballpark. As soon as the gates open Renel Brooks-Moon could be heard on a tape that plays continuously warning fans in attendance not to touch any of the food on the ground because it has been poisoned and should you consume it you will suffer intensely painful and gut wrenching death. I suppose it is inevitable that a few people out of 40,000 in attendance will unwittingly gobble down a piece of poisoned food and endure an excruciatingly painful demise. There is a phrase that fits. It is "collateral damage."

After day one of my "seagull solution" the ballpark would be littered with dead seagull carcasses piled five deep in some places along with an occasional lifeless moronic homo sapien. A positive byproduct would be the increase in the average I.Q. of your typical Giants fan due to the elimination of so many of the most dim-witted and pea-brained of the ballpark attendees. The phrase "addition by subtraction" has never been defined more succinctly.

Days two, three, four, five, six and seven play out in a very similar manner (think "Groundhog Day"). The one exception being (as you can imagine) fewer and fewer seagulls are returning to the park at the conclusion of the game to wolf down an easy meal that is (quite literally) "one the house."

According to my calculations after the seventh day of operation "rid the park of gulls" there would no longer be a single bird present at the conclusion of a ballgame.

As time passes inevitably gulls will be born who never "learned their lesson" about the dangers of eating ballpark food and so the whole scenario would have to be repeated every five years. Eventually it would become the most eagerly anticipated social event on the calendar. The "decimation of the gulls" as it would come to be known would capture the imagination of the entire city. Every five years a huge celebration would take place to coincide with the "cleansing of the park" ritual. Marches, rallies and parties would dot the entire city landscape. Politicians as well as civic and community leaders would speechify from dawn till dusk extolling the virtues of ridding the city of these annoying pests. A three day music festival would be held in Golden Gate Park to be called "hardly strictly strychnine" and would feature many of the top musical acts of the day.

Do not be overly concerned with regards to the financial burden this would place on the Giants organization! Since 2010 the San Francisco baseball club has made obscene amounts of money and (from what I hear) the price of strychnine is at an all-time low.

Three for the Price of One?

I HAVE NOTICED THE RECENT ADDITION OF three new writers in the pages of the Chronicle. Their names are (allegedly) Joe Garofoli, David Talbot and Otris R. Taylor Jr. I find it interesting that the Chronicle would want to hire three writers who share the exact same opinions, politics and world views. It's amazing how many articles I have read of late dealing with "people of color," L.G.B.T.Q. issues, unfair treatment of illegal immigrants, excessive use of force by police officers or how Donald Trump is the root of all evil.

After reading the first sentence of an article written by any of the "three wise progressives" you can fill out the rest of it yourself without the bother of reading further. On the plus side this is a major timesaver while reading the paper. How many times can these three rehash their pet opinions ad nauseam while ignoring all other aspects of the human condition? Thank God for Heather Knight who addresses a variety of subjects that might be of interest to your readers.

I now suspect the Chronicle has shrewdly hired only one person and given him (or her) three names and are using three different bogus photographs to represent the same person. This ingenious money-saving ploy is simply (in my opinion) brilliant. The dead giveaway is the obviously fake photo of Otis R. Taylor Jr. that accompanies his columns. This picture had to be culled from mug shots taken of criminals entering San Quentin Prison. You may be familiar with Edvard Munch's famous artwork "The Scream." I call the photo of Mr. Taylor "The Scowl." He looks like someone who has just received five consecutive life sentences for committing unspeakably heinous crimes for which he feels no remorse whatsoever.

I can hardly wait to read the ultimate article written by this person (or persons). It will no doubt involve an L.G.B.T.Q. "person of color" who is an illegal immigrant and is the victim of excessive force by a police officer. The blame (you guessed it) is placed squarely on the shoulders of Donald Trump.

I was always anxious to read the opinions of Deborah J. Saunders. Though I have never voted for a Republican I was interested in hearing her conservative point of view. It provided a counterbalance to the rest of the Chronicle's uber-progressive slant. I notice her opinions no longer appear in the pages of the Chronicle. I can't help but wonder if she was the victim of a firing or a firing squad.

Bottoms Up

WELL HOORAY, HUZZAH AND HALLELUJAH! THE city of San Francisco is about to be twice blessed. In addition to Senator Weiner's proposal to extend the hours for serving alcohol from 2 a.m. to 4 a.m. city officials and assemblyman Phil Ting D.S.F. are making a push to pass a bill that would create 25 liquor licenses within the city. A few clueless naysayers are insisting these proposals would only serve to "oversaturate San Francisco with alcohol." This claim is patently absurd. Anyone with half a brain knows that San Francisco is already overly saturated with alcohol. So what harm would these proposals possibly do? As for the assertion regarding "undermining public safety" what would you rather have? Public safety or access to alcohol 24/7/365? I rest my case.

This elixir (or panacea) we call alcohol is the answer to virtually all of mankind's problems. Whatever mental, physical or emotional challenges that may beset you copious amounts of alcohol will have you copacetic in "two shakes of a lamb's tail." An extra added benefit of alcohol is how it enhances relationships among one's family and friends. Finding a friend who is mildly amusing, has half a brain and is capable of uttering a coherent sentence or two is like trying to find a needle in a haystack. This is when alcohol is at its most useful. Even the most dull-witted nitwit can appear fascinating and hilarious if one has consumed enough alcohol. Miraculously you are literally rolling on the ground in convulsive laughter at something you would not have found mildly amusing had you not been "three sheets to the wind." Is there a greater joy in life than laughing hysterically at something that isn't even remotely funny? I think not. I doubt if wiser words were ever spoken than "I drink to make you more interesting and amusing."

Though it's true that alcohol is a known carcinogen I say so what. There are hundreds of known carcinogens. Why pick on alcohol? I say let's choose our battles wisely. As for those who classify alcohol as a poison, they remind me of that classic character from children's literature "Chicken Little" who was always saying "the sky is falling." An alarmist worrywart if ever there was one.

While it is true that alcohol related deaths are at an all-time high, so are deaths in general. Since we are all fated to go eventually, why not choose an alcohol related death rather than having to wait around several more decades only to pass on from something as boring and mundane as old age.

The same purveyors of "gloom and doom" insist upon bringing up the negative effects drinking can have on the human liver, being by far the leading cause of cirrhosis. Let's get one thing straight. It is widely known that the liver is the most overrated organs in the entire body, just edging out the second and third most overrated organs; the heart and the brain. Functioning without a liver is now considered "a piece of cake" and many experts now consider the loss of its function to be a "blessing in disguise."

There are only 812 bars and restaurants in San Francisco that have full liquor licenses. Do you realize what this means? It means that in certain parts of the city you could easily traverse a block and a half without passing a place that has alcohol available for purchase. Assemblyman Phil Ting shrewdly points out that if you live in the Sunset District you don't want to "go all the way downtown" to find an establishment selling alcohol. Perhaps someone should point out to Mr. Ting that if one was to journey from the Sunset District to downtown you would likely pass approximately 250 restaurants and bars with alcohol for purchase. Maybe in Mr. Ting's world Taraval Street, California, Noriega, Irving, West Portal, 24th Street, Lincoln Way as well as various other locations between the Sunset District and downtown simply do not exist. This begs the question is Phil Ting merely pretending to be a clueless ignorant imbecile or is he (in fact) the real deal.

I am reminded of the ancient Greek philosopher Diogenes (412-323 B.C.E.) who preached self-control "moderation in all things" and "nothing to excess" as the way to health and happiness. Legend has it that Diogenes would search the city streets at night carrying a lantern in search of an honest man, alas, to no avail. If Diogenes were somehow transported to modern San Francisco he could walk the streets of S.F. on a weekend night with his lamp in search of a sober man (or woman). Unfortunately he would have as little success as he did in finding an honest man.

When Alexander the Great made a pilgrimage to visit the famous philosopher, who was sunning himself on a warm afternoon Alexander said to him "Ask anything you wish and I will grant it if I can." "Please move out of my sunlight" was Diogene's reply. Alexander's response was "If I were not Alexander I would like to be Diogenes."

How to Cope with Shelter-In-Place

WHAT ARE MANY PEOPLE DOING SINCE SHELTER in place has tethered them to their living quarters? Catching up on their reading? Watching educational and informative television programs in an effort to improve their minds? Spending quality time with immediate family members? Learning a new language or watching classic movies on DVD? No doubt some are but what many Bay Area residents are doing is consuming more alcohol. During the first week of S.I.P. Bay Area residents drank 42% more alcohol than usual. Wine.com reports its spirits sales have surged 400% since S.I.P. orders started.

I don't know about you but whatever I feel that I could use some help I immediately reach for a bottle of alcohol (not the rubbing variety, the 100 proof variety). I figure if copious amounts of liquor can't solve my problems what can?

Americans who "drown their sorrows" are on the cutting edge of modern concepts of health care. After all, how much stress are you feeling if you are passed out drunk in an alcohol induced coma? The short answer? None. People who engage in this type of binging often (when they finally come to) find themselves refreshed, energetic, alert and ready to take on the world with a newfound enthusiasm that is difficult (if not impossible) to find outside of a bottle of spirits.

Overindulging has other advantages as well. Boredom can be a problem being stuck at home during the pandemic. How does one pass the time during the long hours of sheltering in place? If enough alcohol is consumed you may find yourself passed out one day and before you know it, voila, four days have passed.

You will also find it difficult (if not impossible) to argue with any of your house-mates if you are barely able to speak, and if you do, your words are unintelligible.

So if you're like me (and so many fellow Americans) you will meet the myriad challenges presented by shelter-in-place orders head on. With a marked increase in your alcohol consumption.

An Ideal Family

We have been so inspired (and amazed) by pride month and the solidarity of the L.G.B.T.Q.I.A. community we have decided that when we are reincarnated and living our next lifetime we will once again find each other, get married and raise a family. Only this time we intend to do it right.

Though we are so happy and proud of how our three boys turned out we cannot escape the nagging thought that somehow we must have gone wrong. To have produced three children, all of whom are heterosexual is (to put it mildly) somewhat of a disappointment and (quite frankly) an embarrassment. Not only did our children have to live with the stigma of having only one mother and one father but to make matters worse their parents are of differing sexes (one a female and one a male). (As you can imagine) all through school our kids were ostracized, ridiculed and generally shamed because of the deplorable family life they were forced to endure.

Not being constantly shuttled between mom and dad's house, not getting to meet dad's new girlfriend (or boyfriend). Not getting to meet mom's new boyfriend (or girlfriend). Not getting to enjoy the status of having two moms or two dads. Children can be so cruel when they see other kids who are "different" such as ours. Their taunts have left a lasting scar on our boys that they are still dealing with to this day.

During our next iteration of parenthood we intended to do it right. Our plan is to have seven children. One lesbian, one gay, one bisexual, one transsexual, one queer, one intersexual and one asexual. In the true spirit of diversity and inclusion; and employing the tactic of adoption we would also prefer that all seven be of different races. One Pacific Islander, one African, one Asian, one Hispanic, one Arab, one American Indian, and one Inuit. No need for another caucasian because if you are not a "person of color" you may as well not be a person at all. While growing up in San Francisco in the 50's and 60's the S.F.U.S.D. was made up of 90% caucasians and 10% other. In 2017 it was 90% other and 10% caucasian. That's what is known as an ideal racial balance. While on a recent walk in the city I spotted a family of five caucasians walking together on a city street. This shocked, amazed and astounded me and so I had to find out what they were doing in our city limits. As it turned out they were on vacation from the Midwest. Simple explanation. The next caucasians I encountered led to an incredible scene. Just as I spotted the unsuspecting pair of caucasians two S.F. public health workers appeared. One took out a tranquilizer gun and shot the two of them with a dart where the sun don't shine. In a matter of seconds they were both immobilized and lying lifeless upon the ground. Quickly the two health officials moved in. The caucasians were then "tagged" with microchips which were implanted behind their left earlobes. This will allow public health officials to track the caucasian's every movement and know their whereabouts at all times. Where they go, what time they eat, which minorities they interact with and (of course) their mating habits will all be closely monitored. This information will be used to try and preserve the few remaining caucasians still living within the city limits.

If current trends do not change soon the only caucasians to be found in San Francisco will be those housed in the S.F. Zoo in the caucasian display area simulating their natural habitat.

The diversity I have described, to my mind, would represent the ideal family. After all, heteros do not celebrate a "pride month," a "pride week," a "pride day," minute, hour or second. Presumably this is because heteros (or breeders, if you will) feel absolutely no pride whatsoever (and deservedly so). In an effort to instill a modicum of pride in the hetero community I am currently spearheading a drive (I am the chair of an ad hoc committee) to create a hetero pride festival. It is to be held during hetero pride nano-second. Some may argue that a billionth of a second is a relatively short period of time for a celebration of this sort. My argument is look how little influence, impact and significance heteros have had on the history of humankind.

We celebrate the accomplishments of George Washington and Abraham Lincoln (combined) for one day in February. Jesus Christ's birth is celebrated for one day in late December. It would appear the significance of L.G.B.T.Q.I.A. community trumps the Lord Savior by 30 times.

Since heteros totally lack pride there is no reason to fly a flag of many colors. Heteros are completely lacking in pink triangles as well. Though I understand there is a groundswell of support and a grass-roots campaign to adopt a chartreuse trapezoid as a representation of hetero pride. Another upside to our amazing family will be the utter joy of having seven children who (hopefully) produce zero grandchildren. As we all know grandchildren are (quite possibly) the most overrated entities on this entire planet. Who (I ask you) needs them? I have come to suspect that virtually all of those grandparents who literally leapt for joy upon hearing of their impending grandparenthood and constantly brag about their grandkids with a huge smile on their face are merely acting as if they are overjoyed and ecstatic over the birth of these new family members. Often this well rehearsed hoax can actually be quite convincing.

We also can't wait to have several family members who refer to themselves in the plural. People have been referring to themselves in the singular for millenia and so I think the time has come to stop perpetrating the asinine notion that a person is an individual and not a group of beings. I personally know several people who are (trust me) a crowd in themselves. While we're at it let's put an end to the usage of such terms as him or her, he or she and man or woman. Gender specific!!! Do you have any idea how many people are offended by these terms? I'll tell you how many. Approximately 0.00000000001 percent of the population at large. So let's put a stop to offending such a humongous slice of our society. Finally I am sick and tired of knowing the sex of a person by hearing that individuals (their) first name. All names should be gender non-specific such as Kramer, It, Thing, Bereavement or Gargantua. The world (it seems) just keeps getting more awesome with every passing day.

Truckers Behaving Badly

Have you ever been driving on the freeway about 70 miles an hour? Up ahead there is a steep grade. There are two lanes and in the right lane are two huge trucks. Due to the hill they are climbing, one of the trucks is going 20 miles an hour and the one behind it is going 21 miles an hour. Just before you are able to fly by the two trucks, one going 21 miles an hour pulls into the left lane causing a backup of cars that had to slow down from 70 miles an hour to 20 miles an hour. The 21 mile an hour trucker could not bear going 20 miles an hour and so had to pass the "slower" truck. Because of how slow the trucks are moving and the extreme length of the vehicles it takes an eternity for the 21 mile an hour truck to finally pass the 20 mile an hour truck and merge back into the right lane. Really? Seriously? Truckers can't go one mile an hour slower until they reach the top of the hill? How stupid, selfish and pig-headed can you be? Stay in the slow lane you dimwitted pea brained fool. How many nano-seconds could you possibly save by slowing down everyone in the fast lane by about 50 miles an hour. These truckers appear to be concerned only with themselves and no one else. In the world of truckers it is preferable to force scores of cars to reduce their speed from seventy to twenty miles an hour than for one truck to have to reduce its speed one mile an hour. This is sometimes referred to as "truckers logic."

A Better World

It SEEMS TO ME THAT MORE AND MORE PEOPLE are worried, concerned and apprehensive about a possible impending nuclear holocaust. I believe the election of our current POTUS, who happens to be a macho cowboy with an itchy trigger finger, bad hair and a belligerent infantile mentality may have something to do with this phenomenon. I will try to allay these fears if I possibly can. If indeed world war three does break out it could prove to be a blessing in disguise.

Many people envision a worst case scenario where the entire planet is destroyed and everything (including all life forms) are totally wiped out. This (I can assure you) will not occur. Humankind, even with all of his weapons of mass destruction could not put an end to this amazing planet. The oceans are too vast, the land masses too formidable and some life forms too hardy to be completely annihilated. After the smoke has cleared, the dust has settled and the blessed winds have blown away the lion's share of the toxic radiation, these practically indestructible things will still exist on planet Earth: 1) Cockroaches 2) Various one celled creatures such as amoebas and protozoans 3) Vinyl records and 4) Female human beings. Wiping out all of the males on our planet is a distinct possibility. Wiping out all of the females? Impossible! These amazing resourceful, highly intelligent, extremely hardy and thoroughly capable beings will find a way to solve any and all problems that are sure to arise after the nuclear armageddon.

Propagation of the human race without any contribution from the male of the species represents a formidable problem. Amongst the many surviving females there are sure to be some surgeons who are skilled at their chosen craft. Finding or making objects sharp enough to perform the necessary operations that will be required should not prove too difficult a task. The most astute of our surgeons will not be daunted by the job of harvesting the sperm from the dead lifeless male corpses that will litter the landscape of the post apocalyptic world. Once this has been done artificial insemanation involving the smartest, cleverest and healthiest of the surviving females can begin in earnest. Soon babies of both sexes will be born and eventually humans can return to breeding the good old fashioned way.

The reintroduction of men into this new world is also a crucial aspect. No doubt in clearing away rubble and making the planet habitable once again numerous heavy objects will have to be lifted and carried from one place to another, thus making the male of the species useful once again.

Since the first incarnation of the human experiment resulted in abject failure and utter calamity it doesn't take much imagination to envision a considerably better world than the one that was totally destroyed. I am confident that when we get a second chance humans will learn to live in peace and harmony for eons to come. Or at least until another macho cowboy with bad hair, an itchy trigger finger and a belligerent infantile mentality is elected president of the world's most powerful nation.

Multitasking to the Extreme

I UNDERSTAND THAT IN ORDER TO SAVE TIME it is occasionally necessary to multitask. That being said I have to think that appearing in a video conference from a traffic violation trial while performing a plastic surgery operation is taking the concept a bit too far.

The medical board of California is investigating Dr. Scott Green for doing just that. It seems that Dr. Green appeared for his Sacramento superior court trial, held virtually due to the coronavirus pandemic, from an operating room. He was dressed in surgical scrubs with a patient undergoing the procedure just out of view. The beeps of the machinery could be heard in the background.

I applaud Dr. Green for "killing two birds with one stone" (as the saying goes) and getting as much done as possible in the time he had available. Many people falsely assume that conducting a surgical procedure requires all the attention and concentration one can muster to do the job properly. Dr. Green has shown us it is simply not so. This could be the start of a whole new trend in the medical profession. Soon adroit brain surgeons will not idle away the several hours it takes to perform complicated brain surgery doing only that. Why not book your next pleasure cruise with Cunard or Princess at the same time? In the midst of open-heart surgery? Time to check the latest scores, stats and highlights on your ESPN app. Surgeons who are reality T.V. fans could have a 75 inch hi def television installed in the operating room. They would not have to miss a single episode of Survivor, Big Brother or The Bachelorette. The possibilities are virtually endless.

I see no reason why female surgeons should forego their scheduled pedicure simply because they happen to be performing an appendectomy. Even eye surgery can be accomplished, with one hand, while chowing down with the other.

Kudos for Dr. Green for opening up a whole new world for surgeons from coast to coast.

Ivermectin Miracle

Like most of my fellow brilliant thinkers I have eschewed the coronavirus vaccine out of fear of fatal, lethal, or even mortal side effects that so commonly accompanies the vaccine (it says so on Facebook). I am, however, totally on board with taking copious amounts of Ivermectin. Ivermectin is usually used to deworm horses. Unfortunately it proved to be totally useless in preventing me from contracting Covid-19.

On the plus side I have never been freer of worms in my life. Interesting side effects include: I now tend to walk on all fours, consume 100 pounds of oats a day and can run a mile in just under two minutes. As an extra added bonus, for some reason, I seem to have more horse-sense than I had before. I can't imagine why.

A Statue of Liberty for San Francisco

THERE HAS BEEN A LOT OF TALK RECENTLY about the rise in certain crimes in San Francisco and the soaring number of homeless within the city limits. Auto break ins are at an alltime high as well as intravenous drug use (often in public) and people with severe mental health issues around every corner. This (to me) makes perfect sense. After all, if one is homeless, a drug abuser (or pusher) or suffers from acute mental problems, where else would you rather be?

In addition to the mild year round climate there are other compelling reasons to head for the "city by the bay." With the "uber liberal" "ultra progressive" political climate that permeates the board of supervisors, city government, the judicial system and the mayor's office nowhere in the country is as welcoming to the aforementioned individuals as San Francisco.

The city is notorious for slapping the wrists of such offenders, giving them ridiculously light sentences, (should they be incarcerated at all) and getting them back on the street as quickly as possible so they can continue their business as usual. How many times have we heard S.F. Police officers speak of making arrests of criminal perpetrators only to see them avoid prosecution and jail time because of San Francisco's ultra liberal courts and judges, leaving many in the S.F.P.D. frustrated and helpless? It has recently been revealed that Nevada has been sending its incorrigibles, mental patients and other undesirables to San Francisco via a one-way bus ticket to our "welcoming" and "inclusive" city. Nevada officials hope the uber tolerant and permissive climate in San Francisco will result in out taking in all these people they don't want living in Nevada. The results of these policies have been a disaster. Who hasn't heard of someone from San Francisco, after returning to S.F. from visiting another city, marvel at how clean the streets were there. The lack of homeless people astounds them. No one shooting up drugs in public. No one using public streets as their personal bathroom. It can be quite a shock to return to San Francisco from a city not beset by all of the ugly problems San Franciscans face on a daily basis.

Another offshoot of liberal progressive San Francisco policies are the multiple deaths that have occured because of sanctuary city policies. People are dying because violent criminals are being shielded from deportation because of failed and flawed sanctuary city policies. J.F.L. Sanchez had been on track for a sixth deportation to Mexico after serving 46 months in prison for felony re-entry into the country, but he was released from the city jail three months before the Pier 14 killing rather than being turned over to federal immigration agents under the city's sanctuary cities law. J.F.L. Sanchez had been transferred from federal custody to the city jail in March 2015 on an old warrant that he fled marijuana charges in 1995. When prosecutors discharged the case the S.F. Sheriff's Department released him despite a federal request to hold him for deportation. This led to Lopez-Sanchez stealing a gun from a park ranger's vehicle, discharging the weapon and killing Kate Steinle in front of her father and family.

More deaths have ensued caused by people who had not been charged with crimes when they should have been or were not deported because of sanctuary cities policy. I suggest we erect a huge Statue of Liberty in San Francisco Bay like the one in New York harbor. It would depict as S.F. Police officer and an I.C.E. federal agent kneeling on the ground with both hands shackled behind their backs rendering them totally unable to do their jobs. The inscription would read "Give us your L.G.B.T.Q.I.A.'s, your homeless, your drug addicted, your drug pushing, your mentally impaired, your runaways, your jobless, your illegal immigrants, your "smash and grab" perpetrators, and your criminals of all kinds yearning to avoid any prosecution or jail time whatsoever. Fear not for San Francisco's ultra liberal progressive lawyers, judges and legal system will do everything possible to make sure you are not held accountable for any transgressions or crimes you have committed. Welcome to San Francisco."

An Open Letter to Mick LaSalle - Chronicle Movie Critic

MICK LASALLE EXPRESSES SURPRISE AND disappointment that an "Oscar calibur" film such as "Manchester by the Sea" performed so poorly at the box office. The reason is quite simple. These "highly regarded" artsy, pretentious, pseudo-intellectual endless slogs are a pain in the ass to sit through.

Perhaps film critics like Mick LaSalle enjoy these boring ordeals so much is that they, like the films they review, are artsy, pretentious pseudo-intellectuals. I picture you and your fellow critics standing around the lobby with one hand in your pocket and the other grasping a glass of white wine discussing the subtle nuances, symbolism and emotional depth the movie conveyed. This (I am sure) leaves your readers extremely impressed with your opinion of what an outstanding film should contain.

The truth is that "Manchester by the Sea" consisted of one boring, vapid scene after another. The dialogue was unbearable (do people really talk to each other that way?). The teenage nephew appears to have an I.Q. of approximately twelve. The conversations between Afleck and his nephew were truly painful. We displayed amazing discipline and sticktoitiveness by not walking out of the theater until the entire dull, drab, tedious mess was over. Correct me if I'm wrong but isn't the whole point of going to the movies (excuse me cinema) to have fun, enjoy yourself and be glad that you came to the show. A good movie can be entertaining, enlightening, amusing, interesting or touching. M.B.T.S. was none of those things.

You lament the paltry box office totals for M.B.T.S. I wonder what the box office would have been had you and your fellow critics not anointed M.B.T.S. a "cinematic masterpiece"? If it had to rely solely on word of mouth recommendations theaters all across America showing M.B.T.S. would have been devoid of human life.

We have been duped and deluded far too often by a positive Mick LaSalle review only to be disappointed by a movie that was not worth seeing. It is time to treat Mick LaSalle like a crazy, sponging annoying relative and simply pretend he does not exist.

My personal favorite Mick LaSalle review was from a few years ago of a movie called "Amour." At the beginning of the review you wrote "This has got to be some kind of great movie." Later in the review you stated that when the director wasn't boring you to death he was torturing you. From this we can only assume that you come to the theater hoping to be bored and tortured (Mick LaSalle, masochist?). What I always wondered is if you're absolutely certain the director wasn't boring you to death and torturing you at the same time?

Teens Need to be Able to Return Fire

POLICE COMMISSIONER JOHN HAMASAKI'S suggestion that it can be dangerous to take guns away from teens because it leaves them unable to defend themselves in their dangerous neighborhoods is (to my mind) spot on. When shots ring out in "low-income communities of color" (as they so often do) the last thing you want is to not have the wherewithal to return fire. This attitude jibes perfectly with the "kill or be killed" mentality that permeates so many of these urban ghettos.

To carry this idea a logical step further, rather than taking guns away from teens it should be mandatory for teens to be armed at all times. When they are in certain high-crime low-income zip codes. To enhance their safety and well-being citations would be issued to teens who are found not in possession of a fully loaded firewarm. Any teen who racked up several citations for "failure to carry a weapon" would be facing a lengthy stint in the state penitentiary (and deservedly so).

Ideally, upon reaching the age of thirteen families would celebrate a "rite of passage" or "coming of age" ceremony where the teen receives his (or her) very first firearm. It would be similar to the Jewish bar or bat mitzvah recognizing a child's passage into adulthood. In the Latin world a quinceanera celebration is held upon a girl's 15th birthday in a similar manner.

Parents, siblings, grandparents and other family members would join in celebrating the child's acquisition of a weapon capable of snuffing out a life with the mere pull of a trigger. Photographs (suitable for framing) would be taken of the beaming youngster proudly displaying their prized possession as the parents look on with pride. At long last they could finally breathe a sigh of relief knowing their child would no longer be weaponless and vulnerable but instead have the firepower to respond in kind if fired upon.

Parents being what they are, it would soon be a source of satisfaction to provide one's child with the latest and most deadly state-of-th-eart weaponry. A kind of friendly competition would (no doubt) emerge. "My kids gun is more powerful, lethal, destructive and dangerous than your kids gun" would emerge as a popular bumper-sticker. "Weapon on board" would be another popular decal along with the image of a machine gun to complete the picture.

In an effort to procure a weapon for one's child, taking out thirty year loans would be necessary to finance the purchase of a high powered bazooka, rocket launcher or (a more affordable option) gatling gun. So let's all get behind John Hamasaki's notion because when shots are fired the more people who are capable of firing back the safer we all will be.

Berkeley Strikes Again

What can you say about the Berkeley City Council uber-progressives? Ultra-politically correct? Or perhaps a group of people intent on finding solutions to problems that don't exist.

The latest example of Berkeley being "ahead of the curve" and "on the cutting edge of modern sensibilities" the city council adopted an ordinance to replace gendered language in municipal code. Personal pronouns like "she," "he," "her," and "him" will be replaced with "they" and "them." It's about time this most crucial change in how we refer to people was adopted. After all, individuals have been referred to in the singular for millennia in virtually all languages all over the globe. I say "enough is enough." Why should we use terms that are applicable for 99% of the population when we can tailor our language to the one percent of our citizens that may (or may not) take offense to such terms.

When I heard of this I immediately decided that I too would like to be referred to in the plural. The problem was I simply could not decide which word I wanted to be known by. Among the words I thought would describe me best were "a host" "a horde" "a veritable plethora" "a myriad" "a slew" "a throng" or "a multitude." I was so torn I simply could not make up my mind. What I did opt to do is to choose a "gender neutral" designation for myself. After all, I can't think of anything worse than being able to discern a person's gender by the sound of their first name. That (to me) would be the very definition of hell. To avoid this dire possibility I gave endless hours of thought about what I would want to be known as so that no one could possibly know my sex until we met in person (and maybe not even then). So I decided that henceforward everyone is to refer to me as "It." I feel that "It" pretty much sums up the persona I want to project and the image I am trying to convey. If one is not comfortable calling me by my chosen name an alternate possibility would be "That thing over there."

I am not sure, however, which gender choice I'm going to choose for the "new me." I believe Facebook now lists 54 gender options for member's profiles. Only three more would equal Heinz 57 varieties. That is a milestone worth shooting for.

I don't recall exactly when the world started to become so complicated, I only know that it has.

Surprise, Surprise

WE WERE TALKING THE OTHER DAY ABOUT how much things have changed in San Francisco from back when we were growing up. If one could have been magically transported from 1960 to today what would surprise you the most? How about the size of modern television screens? People who always have a cellphone in their hands, sleep next to it and suffer from separation anxiety should they misplace it for 15 seconds? The gay, community invading the Castro District?

Does anyone know why San Francisco was anointed the gay capitol of the universe? Why not Des Moines, Iowa? Or Timbuktu, Mali? Better yet how about a distant planet orbiting the star Arcturus in the constellation Bootes? I understand the weather is great there in the fall.

After much thought and consideration I choose for personal favorite change in modern San Francisco, Halloween costumes for adults. Who would have guessed back in the day that Halloween costumes for adults would burgeon into a 500 million dollar a year enterprise? The desire to dress up on Halloween used to completely abate around the time puberty kicked in. No so today. In the fities or sixties if you had a Halloween costume on and were over the age of twelve it meant you had a serious problem. All of your friends (should you have any friends) would be pointing at you and laughing hysterically.

What has changed in America and especially San Francisco? It can be summed up by what I call infantile, permanent-adolescent, shirking syndrome, or

IPASS. Symptoms include delaying (or never) getting married or having children, living alone (would you want to live with a middle-aged adolescent?) and forever behaving like a recent high school graduate. Significantly you can dress up and attend a Halloween party because you have no children to take trick-or-treating.

Rather than a spouse and children, those suffering from IPASS prefer to have a "boyfriend" or "girlfriend." We now see people in their fifties, sixties or even seventies with a "boyfriend" or a "girlfriend." Soon we will have "boyfriends" and "girlfriends" who are pushing a walker (or being pushed in a wheelchair) in an elder-care facility. Most experts agree that the main cause of IPASS is an intense and overwhelming desire to avoid any and all responsibility. There is no known cure for IPASS but doctors all across America are working feverishly to try to discover a cure for this debilitating disease. Experts in the mental health field have noticed a sharp increase in IPASS cases. So if you know someone who participates in the "Santa Skivvies Run," wears some idiotic costume and runs in the Bay to Breakers, can't wait for 4/20 to celebrate smoking weed or considers Halloween their "favorite holiday" (is halloween even a holiday?) recommend an IPASS screening test to them immediately. Immunologists say there could be a vaccine ready by late spring or early fall at the latest. There is hope at last.

What's "Special" and What's "Normal"

WHILE DRIVING PAST LAKESHORE ELEMEN-tary School the other day I remarked to my wife, who taught there for years, how many school buses were parked out in front. "Those are just the "special education" busses" she said. "O.M.G." I said. "There are that many "special ed." kids at Lake-shore? "One semester," she told me, "almost half of my students were identified as "special education."

This got me to thinking. If current trends continue, with more and more people being classified as "special ed.", eventually there will be more "special ed." students than "normal" students.

When this occurs will the "special ed." kids become "normal" and the "normal" students become "special"? It seems to me the majority of the students are ones who are "normal" and something that is "special" has to be in the minority.

I hope when this ironic role-reversal occurs former "special ed." kids do not start making fun of the former "normal" kids because there are so few of them and they just "don't fit in."

Out Antiseptic World

How great is it to be living in San Francisco in the 21st century? Everything is so much better than it was when we were growing up in the 50's and 60's. San Francisco is such an amazing place to live (and die) in.

For decades one could pick up most any newspaper (there used to be several) and turn to the obituaries and read about those who had recently passed away. Not Good. It seems that the time-honored tradition of obituaries simply had to go due to the proliferation of new-age, modern sensibilities. The problem lies with the term "obituary." Negative connotation, (I.E. someone has died). We must avoid negative connotations at all costs. Frequent readers of the Chronicle may have noticed the word obituary has been replaced by the phrase "Life Tribute." Now, isn't that better? Now the connotations are positive. "Life." "Tribute."

How awesome is it to purge the word obituary and replace it with "Life Tribute." Almost makes me want to hurry up and die already so I too can have a tribute in my honor. Though I have never had a tribute paid to me while living it gives me a warm glow all over knowing there is one in my future (or will it be my past?), it makes me want to live a life worthy of a tribute, but I fear it is far too late for that. On the plus side it is clear that everyone receives a tribute whether they deserve it or not.

After the "Life Tribute" it is on to the next phase. Does anyone still remember when we used to have "funerals" to pay our respects to the "dearly departed."

Friends and family members would gather to lament the passing of a loved one. A solemn somber, hushed tone would be the order of the day. Not any more. "A celebration of life" has taken the place of the "funeral." Life celebrations are up beat, fun and positive. After all, why let the death of a close personal friend or immediate family member spoil your whole day? Dry those tears and put a smile back on your face. Who has the time to spend a couple of hours grieving? This could easily (if you're not careful) put a damper on your entire afternoon.

Something else that has disappeared from modern usage is (of course) the janitor. No one has seen "hide nor hair" of a janitor for years. Somewhere along the line "janitors" mysteriously morphed into "custodians." (Did that require a raise in pay?) It seems that this new term was inadequate and instead we now have "sanitary engineers." This new title could help explain why former "janitors" are loath to actually clean up any messes they encounter. Would you expect an engineer to mop up some sick child's barf or unclog a stopped-up toilet? Of course you wouldn't! Many former janitors have not been spotted in the company of a mop for decades. In fact many of them don't even know what a mop looks like. Most school janitors, when presented with a mess to clean up, scatter like cockroaches who have had a light shined upon them. Good luck catching one. When told to clean up or fix something it is amazing how all of a sudden they can neither speak or understand the English language. Amazing.

How can you broach the subject of our antiseptic society without mentioning the "participation trophy," my personal favorite. The "participation trophy" came about because parents of less skilled children were tired of children on winning teams being awarded with trophies while their children had to do without. A new system had to be devised so that every child who participated was rewarded with a trophy, just like the players on the championship team. Previously the idea of trophies was to honor excellence and outstanding performance. It has been determined that mediocrity (or worse) is also worthy of a trophy. Wouldn't want to offend little Johnny (or his parents). What a great message to send to our children. No matter how poorly you perform you will be rewarded just as if you had won. No need to practice so as to get better and improve your skills. Why bother putting in the time and effort? Let's have children grow up thinking everyone wins and no one loses. What a great message to teach our kids.

By shielding our children from all disappointment we are not preparing them for the real world. They are going to be in for a real shock when they find out what life is really like. Overprotective parents who baby their children in such a manner are doing their kids more harm than good.

Gen's Performance

We had the chance recently to see a most interesting film. The movie is called "'68" and was written and directed by a talented filmmaker named Steve Kovacs. It depicts a family's assimilation into American culture against the backdrop of all of the social, political and cultural upheaval taking place at the time. While director Kovacs elicits fine performances from the entire cast one (to me) stands head and shoulders above the rest. Steve's young daughter Genevieve Kovacs, only six years of age at the time, is a revelation during her all too brief screen time. To say that she stole the scene would be a gross understatement. She literally lights up the screen with a natural elegance that many veteran actresses find difficult to achieve. Seldom (if ever) have the words "Mmmmm can I have some too?" been delivered with such panache, elan, poise, aplomb and joie de vivre. Her performance is simply riveting and while Gen is on screen it is impossible to take your eyes off her.

It is difficult to fathom the best supporting actress snub that the Motion Picture Academy unjustly foisted upon Gen and her family. For this viewer the Oscar should have been a slam-dunk no-brainer. Had Gen chosen to pursue an acting career and not opted to go into the law profession I can assure you no one would have ever heard of Meryl Streep. Do yourself a favor and see "'68" and marvel at the tour-de-force performance of an awesome young talent.

Is the Rainbow Flag No Longer Enough?

Is this article by Tony Bravo serious? It sounds to me like a parody, a lampoon, a send-up or a spoof. The big question on Tony Bravo's mind is if Gilbert Backer's rainbow gay pride flag is an "out dated emblem favored by primarily white, cisgendered queer people."

It would appear that people in the LGBTQ community have a lot more to worry about than your typical human being. I rarely (if ever) have time to worry about if there is an acceptable flag to represent me regarding my gender or sexual affiliation. You have no idea how much easier it is to sleep at night without these life-defining issues burdening my consciousness from dawn till dusk.

In August 2020 the LGBTQ newspaper The Bay Area Reporter suggested that a more "inclusive" version of the rainbow flag should be installed at Market and Castro. A "progress pride flag," a rainbow designed by Daniel Quasar in 2018 that includes the transgender flag colors and black and brown stripes was suggested. Perhaps the answer lies in erecting more flag poles in order to honor as many "communities" as possible to achieve a heightened sense of inclusion. Among the flags that should be proudly flown at Castro and Market would include the asexual pride flag, bisexual flag, intersex pride flag, lesbian pride flag, nonbinary pride flag, pansexual pride flag, Philadelphia pride flag, progress flag, straight ally flag, transgender pride and the two spirit pride flag.

Most doctors and health care specialists are in agreement that the excessive amount of headaches so many people in the LGBTQ community are suffering from is primarily being caused from excessive thinking, constantly worrying about being disrespected and taking life, themselves, their sexual orientation, which one of Facebook's fifty-four gender options to choose (today), if a statue, work of art, book, movie or play offends them and just about anything else you can think of way too seriously. How can you possibly enjoy life when you are constantly distracted by fretting over all of these possible slights (real or imagined) and whether or not they are being properly represented by an appropriate flag? Why not try living life simply as a human being and not a gender, sexual orientation or a race, color or creed? Can life possibly be as complicated as these people who are so concerned about flags in the Castro make it out to be? Life is too short to be obsessed over what flag (or flags) should be flown in the Castro. Perhaps they should try "giving it a rest" for a while.

"My People" Will Talk to "Your People"

Dear Gen

I am ecstatic at the possibility of "my people" getting in touch with "your people." However (to be perfectly honest) "my people" is (in reality) "my person." I have to add that no one has seen hide nor hair of "my person" for decades. Apparently he was so ashamed of being "my person" that he went into the federal witness protection program and had dropped off the face of the Earth and refuses to show his face in public in fear of the ridicule, humiliation and scorn that would be heaped upon him. No doubt he is living under a nom de plume in an effort to disguise his true identity. If this coward can be located and flushed out I will have him get in touch with "your people" toot sweet. Rumor has it he is living in a yurt somewhere outside of Ulaanbaatar, Mongolia where he ekes out a livelihood milking yaks.

Texans Want to Purge
Gun Restrictions

With the latest shooting leaving ten people dead, gun control advocates are clamoring for tighter restrictions for gun ownership.

In Texas they have chosen another direction. Lawmakers there are in the process of removing one of its last major gun restrictions. They have approved laws allowing people to carry handguns without a license and the background check and training that go with it. The Republican dominated legislature approved the measure sending it to Governor Greg Abbot who has said he will sign it.

Texans understand how crucial it is for virtually everyone to be "armed and dangerous" at all times. You never know when someone might offend you in some way. Should this occur you want to be able to produce a loaded firearm post-haste (before you have a chance to cool down) and put a bullet between the eyes of your tormentor. Should you (God forbid) only manage to wound your adversary he (or she) would have the opportunity to return fire (which is only fair) and blow you to smithereens.

A loaded firearm can come in handy in any number of situations. Have you ever been in a twelve items or less line at the grocery store and the person in front of you obviously has more than a dozen items to be checked. This (to me) would be an ideal time to whip out your gun of choice and start blasting away. It's time we put a stop to scofflaws violating express line limits. Most Texans would also agree being cut off on the road or a disputed parking space at the local convenience store represents a perfect opportunity to let loose with a barrage of bullets.

It is unclear if it is merely a coincidence or something that residents of the Lone Star State do intentionally but the vast majority of Texans prefer a caliber of firearm that matches their I.Q. It just so happens that most Texans have an I.Q. of between 22 and 45 giving them several options to choose from.

Another advantage of firearm proliferation is that should some kind of dispute arise, there is no need to sue, hire a lawyer or attempt to navigate the incomprehensible labyrinth of our court system. Simply pull out your "peacemaker" of choice and settle the problem on the spot.

Jump in the Air Comedown in Slow Motion?

ONE OF THE MOST TALENTED R&B ARTISTS OF the early 1960's was Gary U.S. Bonds (real name Gary Anderson). His first hit record was called "New Orleans" which reached No. 6 on the pop charts in October of 1960. His biggest hit was "Quarter to Three" which spent two weeks in the number one slot on Billboard's Hot 100 in June of 1961. The song is derived from the music from "A Night With Daddy G" by a group called "The Church Street Five." Both "A Night With Daddy G" and "The Church Street Five" are referenced in the lyrics of "Quarter to Three."

In April of 1962 the song "Twist, Twist Senora" got to the number nine spot on the charts and the lyrics of the song have been haunting me since I heard them when the song first came out. Songwriting credit is ascribed to Guida, Royster, Barge and Legrand. In it they pose this fascinating scenario:

"I want a pretty girl to assist me

Go with me on a twist spree

And in case she gets a notion

I want her to

Jump in the air, come down in slow motion."

What is suggested here (as you may know) is considered impossible by the laws of both physics and gravity. Although perhaps in one of the eleven alternate universes predicted by "String Theory" the laws of physics and gravity are totally different than those found on Earth. An even more bizarre occurrence (to my mind) would entail jumping in the air in slow motion and coming down in real time. Either way, if successful you would be managing a feat seldom (if ever) accomplished in the history of our planet. Accomplishing this feat gives us all something to aspire to. I've got jumping in the air and coming down in realtime down pat. It's the coming down in slow motion that's got me pulling out what little hair I have left. It may be time to give up this pursuit and get back to trying to jump over the moon. I figure if a cow can do it, so can I.

"Last Call for Alcohol"

What's not to like about Scott Weiner's proposal to allow bars and restaurants to serve alcohol until 4 a.m. rather than 2 a.m.? A recent U.S.A. today piece states that health experts now recommend that people should consume no more than one twelve ounce serving of beer, or one four ounce serving of wine, or one one ounce serving of hard liquor per day. I am confident that your typical bar patron who hangs around until the new 4 a.m. "Last Call" will not be exceeding these recommended guidelines. Does Scott Weiner care at all about the health and wellbeing of the citizens of San Francisco and negative long-term ramifications of his proposal? Or is he simply a talking-head/mouthpiece who chatters and panders to bars and restaurants, who charge obscene amounts of money for the alcohol they sell.

If there is one thing we can all agree on it's that Americans in general (and San Franciscans in particular) do not consume enough alcohol. Senator Weiner's bill would go a long way toward correcting this deplorable situation. How can one achieve the desired state of inebriation if limited to a 2 a.m. last call? Many veteran sots are "just getting started" to guzzle their favorite libations at the 2 a.m. closing time. Extending the "last call" to 4 a.m. will surely relieve some of the pressure currently felt to consume as many "adult beverages" and get "drunk off one's ass" as quickly as possible.

Who could have a problem with overconsumption of a substance that makes people talk and act like a nitwit, babble incoherently, become extremely belligerent before hopping into their cars and killing and maiming innocent victims? Causing one's spouse to seek the counsel of a divorce lawyer is often an added benefit.

Being allowed to "knock down shots" until 4 a.m. will further allow San Franciscans to consume even more of a known carcinogen and a substance many health experts have labeled a "toxic poison."

Perhaps Mr. Weiner could sponsor a companion bill that would require most (if not all) employers to start their workers shifts shortly after 4 a.m. That way over imbibers could stumble out of their favorite "watering hole," hop into their "bumper cars" and head straight for work without having to endure the pesky nuisance of having to go home and sleep for a few hours before reporting to work.

Of course alcohol related deaths would experience an inevitable uptick but as Scrooge so aptly put it, this would serve to "decrease the surplus population." I prefer to see the glass (of alcohol) as half full rather than half empty. Cheers!

Say Goodbye to San Francisco

We recently relocated to San Francisco from Truth or Consequences New Mexico. What can you say about a city that was named after a game show? During our first night in the city our car was broken into, the passenger door window was smashed to bits and hundreds of tiny pieces of glass littered the sidewalk. Everything of value had been stolen. It happened right outside of our 3 thousand dollar a month studio apartment. We sold our car and bought a $500.00 bicycle. Two days later the bike was stolen from where it was parked outside of work. The chain lock had been severed with some kind of hacksaw. All the police had to say is that these kinds of crimes are almost never solved. That may be because the police almost never make any attempt to solve them.

I decided to take Uber, Lyft or a cab to work. Unfortunately downtown traffic was so horrendous the two mile journey took an hour and forty-five minutes and cost me $74.95. It seemed to me a bus would make the most sense. After it arrived a half-hour late I was packed on to the bus like a sardine in one of those airtight cans. Upon arriving at work I noticed my wallet had been stolen. I finally decided what could possibly go wrong if I walked to work through The Tenderloin district. On day one I walked over and around numerous homeless people who lay scattered along the sidewalks. Most appeared to be asleep or dead (I couldn't tell which). Others offered to sell me "buds," whatever that is. Next came the drug addicts shooting up in broad daylight. Though the hookers

(I have to admit) were tempting, I was already late for work. The aroma of urine and solid excrement wafted through the air. A block and a half before I reached my job I was mugged and left in the back of an alley. The next day we decided we had enough of living in "paradise" and so we hitch-hiked back to Truth or Consequences and civilization.

"Hell is Other People"

As the great Irish singer, songwriter and musician Van Morrison reminded us in his song "Goin Down to Monte Carlo," sartre (Jean Paul 1905-1980) said that "Hell is other people." Mr. Morrison went on to add "I believe that most of them are." This may seem like a harsh assessment but if you have encountered some of the same people I have, referring to them as hell is letting them off easy. Some people I've met make hell seem like a "day at the beach" (if not "a walk in the park") in comparison. I'm not trying to imply there are people out there who make the devil seem like Mother Teresa. I'm stating it for a fact. You must avoid these people as if your very life depended on it, which (in extreme cases) it just might. Who the hell begat these people I have no idea but somehow many (unfortunately) reached adulthood. Some are simply evil. Others are extremely stupid. It is when the two are combined that you have serious problems.

Some are not quite malignant enough to be referred to as hell. Purgatory perhaps, maybe even limbo but not hell. Try to cultivate friendships with bright, sharp people (if any can be found). Finding one is like trying to find a particular grain of sand in the Sahara Desert, a single drop of water in the Pacific Ocean or writing a one thousand page novel without using the letter "E." Or maybe even harder.

Don't get me wrong. There are many people out there who are well worth knowing, are fine upstanding citizens and have a good head on their shoulders.

Apparently they are not worth writing about in our local newspaper, are never talked about on the evening newscast and most magazines simply aren't aware they exist.

Hopefully, hell is not all other people, merely most other people.

Regarding "Daylight Savings Time Needs to Be Stopped"

THE AUTHOR OF THIS LETTER CAN'T POSSIBLY be serious. Having to modify one's sleep schedule to lessen the effects of the switch to daylight savings time? Complaining about "Circadian rhythm" being out of whack? Several days of sleep deprivation, inefficient work habits and possible health issues? All because of setting his clock ahead one hour in the spring and back one hour in the fall? How hard could that possibly be? I have been conducting this ritual for decades and have (amazingly) suffered no ill effects.

What if this person took a cross-country flight from San Francisco to New York? Would a lengthy stay in a hospital be required after traversing three time zones? Following his release from the hospital several months of bed rest along with physical therapy might be in order. At this point lingering effects of jetlag would have to be dealt with along with chronic bouts of insomnia. Passing through one time zone can subject you to a world of hurt, but three time zones? At the same time? That would be tantamount to taking your life in your hands.

After approximately one year of convalescence our intrepid traveler would be ready for the return flight to San Francisco.

Something's Burning, Man

In modern America there are countless ways an individual can demonstrate their total lack of an IQ. What if (for example) someone came up with the dumbest, most pointless, idiotic and aburd idea one could possibly think of. How many people would blindly follow, convinced that they are part of a new-age movement with cosmic implications? At last count that would be about 70,000.

This simple (yet profound) concept was to make an image of a man, take it to the beach, and burn it. Why hadn't this breakthrough idea been thought of before? It is because in the past you could not find enough sheep (disguised as human beings) who, upon hearing about his endeavor, think to themselves "I simply must become a part of this movement." In fact these days it is no problem finding thousands of people that can be convinced that building a man and burning it is not a total waste of one's time.

This ritual became so popular that a larger venue was required. I've got it. How about Nevada's Black Rock Desert! Black Rock Desert had been shunned and avoided for centuries (if not millennia) so it's sure not to be crowded. Most God forsaken hot hell holes, where daytime temperature in the summer can exceed 110° F are sparsely populated (as a general rule). Burning Man adherents felt this would be the perfect setting to spend 9 ½ days. If you intend to contemplate your navel for 9 ½ days it is best done in temperatures that exceed three digits.

If you bother to familiarize yourself with the 10 principles of Burning Man (but why would you?) you will be subjected to some of the most blatant new-age bullshit psycho-babble ever contrived by the human (presumably) mind. First we have "radical inclusion." (1) Radical inclusion (as opposed to orthodox inclusion) simply means that radicals (free and otherwise) are to be included. After if one dares to include it is best accomplished radically (or not at all). Inclusion of the normal variety simply does not cut it at Black Rock Desert. Here, if something is worth doing at all it's worth doing radically. The implication also implies aliens from all corners of the galaxy will be welcomed with open arms. Carbon based lifeforms or otherwise. Black Rock Desert is even more inclusive than San Francisco (if that's possible).

Next we have (2) gifting. Giving gifts is strongly encouraged at burning man. The "fly in the ointment" however is that receiving gifts is expressly forbidden at the festival. Violation of this ordinance will result in stinging slaps on both wrists and confiscation of your "I survived burning, man!" t-shirt. The net result of this paradoxical law is the presence of gifts everywhere you look lying unopened upon the ground. No horses, however, are ever gifted at burning man for (as you know) it is simply unacceptable to "look a gift horse in the mouth."

Now we come to (3) decommodification (one of the most used words in the dictionary, right after the, it and set). This statute forbids any commercial sponsorships or advertising. No doubt businesses and companies all across America are in mourning because they cannot capitalize on the huge commercial potential of Burning Man.

(4) Radical self-reliance.

If you are planning to attend Burning Man, self-reliance is indeed a key. After trying desperately to convince a spouse, loved-one, friend (or arch enemy) to go with you to a God-forsaken hot hell-hole for 9 ½ days (and failing miserably) you are definitely going to have to rely on yourself. After all, since you are stupid enough to attend "Burning Man" how likely is it that you know someone equally stupid as you are? The odds are (quite literally) astronomical.

(5) Radical self expression.

Are we beginning to see a pattern here? At Burning Man even self-expression is done radically. What I want to know is who the hell else are you going to express but yourself? Your third cousin twice removed? Unless (of course) your mind and body has been usurped by some sinister entity and you have become an unwilling mouthpiece for its evil, nefarious schemes. (I hate when that happens).

(6) Communal effort.

Everyone is expected to do his or her part at Burning Man. Just what everyone is supposed to do is not specified but everyone is supposed to do something. Anyone caught doing nothing will be assigned a task toot sweet. These may include peeling potatoes, cleaning a latrine or dog-sitting someone's pet. "Idle hands are the Devil's workshop" in the desert. Many have perfected the art of looking busy while doing absolutely nothing (just like they do at work). Since there is absolutely nothing to do at Burning Man this last principle can be the most difficult to follow.

(7) Civic responsibility.

It is required that all attendees be responsible civically. If one is responsible un-civically (or civically irresponsible) all hell can break loose (for obvious reasons). This is to be avoided at all costs. The tacit implication here (obviously) is that if you arrived at Burning Man via a Honda Civic you are responsible for all gas purchases, upkeep, lube, oil and filters, filling the tires with air as well as tire rotation, checking all fluid levels, the radiator, the mirror (side and rear view), the transmission, the breaks, not to mention a viable air-freshener. Needless to say if your vehicle is not a civic, you are not responsible.

(8) Leaving no trace.

It would seem that leaving no trace does not include the tons of trash, garbage, debris, litter, refuse, rubbish and waste that are inevitably created when 70,000 people (who are obviously not thinking clearly, if at all) are gathered together in one place. What they are not leaving a trace of (I am sure) I have no idea.

(9) Participation.

This principle speaks to a radical participatory ethic. Is anything done at Burning Man that is not done in a radical fashion? Even participation ethics are done radically. If one attends Burning Man and thinks they can just kick back and not participate then they have (as the saying goes) "another think coming." Not only are you expected to participate (in what?) you are expected to do it in a radically ethical manner. Since the words radical and ethical have pretty much the exact opposite meaning this could pose quite a problem. To be ethical "Being in accordance with the accepted principles that govern the conduct of a profession" and radical "Departing markedly from usual or customary; extreme" at the same time might require one to be a contortionist.

(10) Immediacy.

"Immediate experience is, in many ways, the most important touchstone of value in our culture. We seek to overcome barriers that stand between us and a recognition of our inner selves, the reality of those around us, participation in society, and contact with a natural world exceeding human powers. No idea can substitute for this experience." Really? Seriously? There is no need to mock these words because they mock themselves. That quote raises new-age gibberish, psycho-babble, meaningless, nonsensical, pretentious, ludicrous horseshit to a whole new level. The words (I assume) are purposely incomprehensible in order to fool Burning Man devotees into thinking there is an actual reason to attend when (in reality) there is none. There are people who need something to believe in. Why one would choose to believe in erecting a man, then burning it (I'm sure) I have no idea.

A Stable Genius?

I COMPLETELY AGREE WITH PRESIDENT TRUMP that he is a stable genius. It is widely known that he has been shoveling copious amounts of horse manure at the American people since he began his campaign for the presidency. The fact that he duped enough gullible voters to buy the excrement he was selling does indicate a perverse form of genius.

Not since Heracles was tasked to clean the Augean Stables, which had not been washed out for ages, has anyone seen a more disgusting sight than the one Donald Trump has made of our country. Perhaps several rivers could be diverted through the U.S. to wash away the mess created by our president.

Wondering Where the Lions Are

JUST LIKE BRUCE COCKBURN I OFTEN FIND myself "wondering where the lions are." If you want to survive (and who doesn't?) it can be crucial (if not essential) to know (should any happen to be in your immediate vicinity) precisely where the lions are and (conversely) where they are not. Knowing their exact location can be lifesaving information should you wish to avoid providing a lion with its evening meal.

In his song "When I Paint My Masterpiece" Bob Dylan tells us the hours that he spent inside the coliseum were concerned mostly with "dodging lions and wasting time."

It would seem that Mr. Dylan did not have to wonder where the lions were considering they were right in front of him one must assume that he did not dodge lions and waste time simultaneously. Wasting time while dodging lions would prove a challenge for even the most agile nobel laureate. Later he tells us "Oh those mighty kings of the jungle, I could hardly stand to see 'em." This line indicates that Mr. Dylan is keenly aware that one is in mortal danger when face to face with the "king of beasts," and is (no doubt) plotting some kind of emergency escape route. Apparently he made it out alive.

In their classic oldie from 1961 "The Lion Sleeps Tonight" (No. 1 pop charts for three weeks in November of that year) the Tokens remind us that (fortunately) they spend a great deal of their time (up to 20 hours a day) asleep. It would seem that the male lions become exhausted watching the female lions hunt, kill prey and drag the dead antelope carcasses back to lay before their feet. Naturally the males get to eat first and (of course) consume "the lion's share," hence the popular phrase. Apparently women are not closer to equal rights in the lion's society than they are in human society.

This brings us to the strange and unusual case of "The Cowardly Lion." Many of you are familiar with "The Wizard of Oz," the superb film of 1939 that has been enjoyed by both children and adults for generations. No doubt you can recall the scene when Dorothy Gale, the Tin Woodsman and The Scarecrow first encountered the Cowardly Lion. They are greeted with a show of false bravado and macho posturing which belies his true nature of cowardice. When Dorothy becomes annoyed at the lion's menacing threats to her defenseless dog Toto, she smites the lion right on his snout with the flick of the wrist. Incredulously this action precipitates a crying jag during which the Cowardly Lion is simply inconsolable. An over-the-top reaction if ever there was one. The lion (of course) proceeds to atone for his meek and gutless behavior and redeems himself with timely acts of courage and valor and, as Shakespeare so aptly put it, "All's Well That Ends Well."

The More (Cartridges) The Merrier

I SEE IN TODAY'S PAPER THAT AN APPEALS court took steps toward reviving California's voter approved ban on possessing large capacity gun magazines. The law seeks to limit gun magazines to no more than 10 cartridges. This type of weapon has often been used in mass shootings and has little to do with the 2nd amendment. The NRA is fighting the proposed ban on high capacity magazines. That (to me) is a no brainer. Try to see this issue from the perspective of your typical mass murderer.

When one is endeavoring to bring about as much death, destruction, mayhem, carnage and bloodshed as is humanly possible in as little time as you can, who has the time to reload? In the midst of a senseless murder spree time is of the essence. Time spent reloading one's weapon of choice has a negative effect on your "kill rate." Even the most bloodthirsty homicidal maniac's ability to extinguish the lives of unsuspecting victims drops practically to nil while having to reload. Having one's style cramped in such an annoying manner would be most distressing to even the most hardened "mass executioner."

No need to put this "killing machine" in a bad mood. Should this occur the possibility of him having a hissy-fit rears its ugly head. I say him realizing that almost all mass murderers have been men. It is safe to say that, regarding snuffing out multiple lives in "one fell swoop," women simply "don't get it" (no offense intended). It would appear that the subtle nuances required to master the art of acting as if you were "evil incarnate" seems to have eluded the "fairer sex."

Perhaps the crucial role women play in the birth and nurturing of our next generation of men and women deter them from wiping out large groups of human beings.

It is imperative that everly deranged lunatic with half a brain and a persecution complex have access to a "weapon of mass destruction" so that he can exact revenge on innocent victims and relieve some of his frustration. The high capacity firearm is crucial to making this dream become a reality.

More Gender Bending

What an amazing idea to have a same-sex production of the classic musical "Oklahoma" where both Curly and Laurey are played by women. Why not, in the spirit of "modern sensibilities," have ground breaking productions of the master playwright William Shakespeare's works? Many of his plays are among the most produced on the planet and several could use a modern update to appeal to today's audiences.

I would start by suggesting a lesbian version of the bard's tragic story of star-crossed lovers called "Julia and Juliet." No need for a male to complicate the plot unnecessarily. His timeless "battle of the sexes" "The Taming of the Shrew" would become a battle of the sex in our version. A highlight of the play would come in act IV when Petruchio utters those famous words "kiss me Nate." Isn't it about time for a woman to take on such roles as King Lear or Julius Caesar? How about a lesbian version of the "Six wives of Henrietta the Eighth"?

Cleopatra being portrayed by a woman has (to my mind) gotten old and tired. I would call our new reworking "Antony and Marc." Marc would meet an untimely end when bitten by a poison snake right on his asp.

A reworking of some of the old biblical stories (it seems to me) might be in order. What pious devout Christian could possibly have a problem with an updated version of the tale of the Garden of Eden? His or her children would (no doubt) sit in rapt attention listening to the story of "Adam and Steve." I'm sure this new version would resonate throughout the entire Christian world.

Perhaps the part of the snake could be played by a ferret. Species bending anyone?

"We Are All Impressed"

IT SEEMS LIKE EVERY OTHER DAY YOU PICK UP the newspaper there is yet another daredevil feat of endurance that has been undertaken by some nitwit with nothing better to do than to try and impress the hell out of us with their amazing accomplishments (or failure). No less than three times in recent memory someone has started out from California in some sort of water-craft in an effort to sail, paddle or row across the Pacific Ocean. All three had to be rescued by the coast guard costing the taxpayers of California hundreds of thousands of dollars, but not costing themselves a red cent. Unlike most things in life, having your life saved by the coast guard comes free of charge. It is all worth it as long as they spell your name right in the newspaper.

The latest example has to be one of my favorites. Ultra-runner Timothy Olson is claiming a new speed record on the Pacific Crest Trail by running the 2,650 miles in 51 days, 16 hours and 55 minutes. How many fractions of a second were used (at the time of this writing) remains unclear.

The Pacific Crest Trail runs from the Mexican border to Canada. On Friday morning Olson's family was still waiting for him to emerge from the woods. His family tell us he is physically exhausted, (ya think!) having run the equivalent of back-to-back marathons every day since he set out June 1st. So! I too have run the equivalent of back-to-back marathons. Of course it took me from the Spring of 1954 until January 12th 2019 but, as they say, "Slow and steady wins the race."

All of these daredevil endurance feats have become old, boring and trite. It's time for some new challenges to emerge lest we are all bored to death from the same old same old.

One exploit that might provide a challenge would be to walk from San Francisco to New York on one's hand while juggling a volleyball with your feet. A judicious use of one's time if you ask me.

Surfing the Banzai Pipeline in Haleiwa, Hawaii on Oahu's North Shore has attracted big wave aficionados for decades (if not centuries). In an effort to ride these formidable waves most prefer to use some sort of surfboard. Though difficult, to be sure, the feat has grown tiresome over time and now falls under the heading "What else can you show me?" Why not ditch the surfboard and try and ride the famed pipeline on a popsicle stick? This could only be accomplished on one's tiptoes thereby combining the disciplines of ballet and surfing.

By now we realize that scaling Mt. Everest has been done to death. It has gotten so bad that the litter and trash on the mountain is in danger of becoming an environmental disaster. To combat this worsening problem a law must be passed that requires everyone wishing to make an ascent of the famed peak would have to do so in the dead of winter without a stitch of clothing on (or "starkers" as the Brits say). In addition sherpas would no longer be allowed to assist any climber. The feat would have to be accomplished on a "do it yourself" basis. In time (I assure you) the pollution problem on Everest would be a thing of the past.

My personal favorite might be crawling across the entire length of the Sahara Desert on hands and knees during the hottest months of the year without consuming a single drop of water. Hydrating before the outset, however, would be allowed.

Many of us have seen video of people climbing up the sheer walls of Half-Dome in Yosemite Valley in California. What else is new? Have you noticed you never see video of someone starting at the top and climbing down Half-Dome to the valley floor? Where is Spiderman when you need him?

These are merely suggestions for challenges for our macho supermen to take on in order for them to leave us impressed and in awe.

Aren't Animals Waterproof?

HAVE YOU EVER WONDERED WHY, IF YOU happen to own anything made out of leather, everyone warns against wearing it in the rain or even getting it wet at all because water will ruin the leather and render your garment useless? How can this possibly be? Isn't leather made from the skin of animals? Don't animals often spend all day in the rain (and sometimes half the night) without any ill effects to their hide? To put it another way, aren't animals waterproof? If so, how can water be so toxic to leather? Apparently no one knows.

People have known how to make leather since prehistoric times. The ancient Egyptians made such durable leather that specimens over 3,000 years old have been discovered in almost perfect condition. It would seem that during this 3,000 year period no water came into contact with this Egyptian leather or it would have been completely ruined.

"Surfs Up"

OF ALL THE SONGS WRITTEN BY BRIAN WILSON of the Beach Boys, one of the most intricate, complex and hauntingly beautiful melodies has to be a song titled "Surf's Up" (music by Brian Wilson, Lyrics by Van Dyke Parks). The song concludes by repeating one of my favorite phrases, "The child is the father of the man."

The phrase is taken from the poem "My Heart Leaps Up" by British poet William Wordsworth.

"My heart leaps up when I behold

A rainbow in the sky

So was it when my life began

So is it now I am a man

So be it when I shall grow old

Or let me die!

The child is father of the man"

The words are generally interpreted to mean that man (or woman) is the product of traits and behavior developed in youth. Our family environment, how we are raised by our parents, the values we are instilled with in childhood and the conduct we see around us go a long way in shaping the adult that we become. I implore anyone who takes on the daunting yet rewarding challenge of raising a child to try and remember "The child is father to the man."

An Idea Whose Time Has Come
(And Gone)

In 1996 THE OAKLAND (CALIFORNIA) SCHOOL
board passed a resolution which called for "Ebonics" or "African American Vernacular English" to be recognized as a language with the idea of teaching it in the Oakland School District. The Oakland school board maintained that AAVE was the "primary language" of its majority African American students. Many institutions, however, regard AAVE as a broken and grammatically incorrect variation of standard English. Maya Angelou found the 1996 Oakland school board resolution "very threatening."

Some critics see ebonics (or Black speech) as a sign of limited education and a legacy of slavery. If used as a primary form of speech it is often seen as an impediment to socio-economic advancement. Ya think?

With African Americans lagging behind their Caucasian and Asian counterparts economically why not create an even greater income gap by recognizing, encouraging and teaching a "language" that simply is nonexistent in the world of education, business, science, art, mathematics, medicine, technology, law, religion, economics, finance and government. Seemed like a good idea at the time Oakland School Board?

God knows Blacks have enough impediments to succeeding in our society without throwing more roadblocks in their way.

Examples of Ebonics include dropping the final consonant of words like past (pas) hand (han) or bath (baf). Apparently my two-year-old grandson has been speaking Ebonics for months. He takes a "baf" almost every night.

Other instances can be found in rhythm and blues music. In August of 1955 rock and roll founding father Chuck Berry had a huge hit with the classic R&B tune Maybellene (No. 5 on the pop charts). Berry's first single resonated with both Black and White record buyers which is exactly what this brilliant crossover artist was shooting for. In the lyrics Berry asks "Maybellene, why can't you be true? You "done" started back doin' the things you used to do." Inserting the word "done" into the lyric gives the line more punch and verve. Later in the song he tells us that "It "done" got cloudy and started to rain." The beat and rhythm of the song flows more effectively with the addition of the world "done" added to it.

One of my favorite "Afro" slang phrases used so often in R&B music has to be "Lookie here." It is used simply if the speaker wants you to listen and pay attention to what he or she has to say. The phrase is used by so many artists it would be pointless to try and list them all but (in my opinion) the man who used it most effectively would have to be the "Godfather of soul" AKA "The hardest working man in show business," James Brown. The phrase "Lookie here" echoes through many of the soul masters recordings, to great effect. While Black slang, argot or jargon will continue to be used in African American neighborhoods across the country it is myopic and shortsighted to try and declare it a language and teach it in school.

I have yet to hear of the Brooklyn Unified School District proposing teaching "Pig Latin" or declaring it a real language. "Igpay atinlay" is a form of Latin-esque gibberish. I say "icksnay" to Pig Latin being declared a language and those who disagree should "amscray" post-haste.

Brooklynese doesn't qualify as well. Pronouncing them, those and these as dem, doze and deez simply doesn't cut it in the world of academia.

"Secret languages" that can be understood by a particular group of individuals have been around for ages. The Irish have been speaking a form of English that can only be understood by the native Irish for centuries.

Why Tour? Are You Kidding?

WITH THE EXCEPTION OF OUR FIRST VISIT TO Europe all of our subsequent trips have been tours or crises. The reasons for this are quite simple. Suppose you fly to Paris, London or Rome or any of a number of amazing places in Europe and you stay there for three weeks getting to know "The City of Light" as thoroughly as possible. Over the course of three weeks you can explore this beautiful city extensively, immerse yourself in French culture, see many of the sights and meet a few of the locals. Of course becoming friends with a native Frenchman would require finding someone who doesn't hate Americans with a passion. This could present a problem. After flying back to America, when asked: where did you go in Europe? Your reply is "Paris." Contrast this with a three week tour we went on through "Insight Vacations." Ten countries in 19 days including England, France, Belgium, The Netherlands, Germany, The Check Republic, Hungary, Austria, Italy and Switzerland. Of course some of these countries we were only in a day and a half, but does it really matter? The whole purpose of visiting Europe in the first place is impressing family, friends (and total strangers) with how well traveled you are and to brag about all the places you've seen. If you have ever experienced a "travel snob" you'll know exactly what I'm talking about. What (I ask you) is more impressive? Three weeks in Paris or 10 countries in 19 days? I think the answer is pretty obvious. This type of trip jibes perfectly with our travel philosophy. When in doubt we choose quantity over quality every time. Just to be able to say you've been somewhere is the goal of your savvy traveler. Even if you slept through the entire three hours it took your tour bus to traverse Montengio, Slovakia or some other "off the beaten path" country in Europe. The problem is actually remembering you were ever there at all. No matter, technically you were there and it counts when adding up the countries you have "visited." There is no rule that says one must experience an overnight stay to have seen a country (or even had your eyes open while on the bus passing through). Being physically there is all that is required for you to qualify for (quite literally) "bragging rights."

In a society where "image is everything" and what you post on the internet is so crucial to making people jealous of your amazing life, 10 counties and 17 cities in 19 days will inspire more "likes" on Facebook than three weeks in Paris, London or Rome. Trust me. After all, isn't amassing likes on Facebook what it's all about? Picking up a spoon or some other memento while at a bus-stop tourist trap is highly recommended to further solidify your travel experience. Your vacation only lasts three weeks but the post-trip gloating can last a life-time. So emphasize quantity over quality when vacationing. You may not enjoy the trip nearly as much as you could have but you'll enjoy the post- vacation decades a whole lot more.

Where Graffiti "Artists" Can Stick Their Graffito

Ever wonder why the word graffiti (plural) is always used and the word Graffito (singular) is never used? It is because graffiti "artists" never produce only one drawing or inscription at a time. Their "works of art" are so crucial, so relevant, so essential that several at a time simply must be produced. What baffles me is looking up and seeing graffiti where it would appear that no human being could possibly access, without risking their life and limb to achieve their goal of making the city landscape even uglier than it already was (if that's possible). Freeway overpasses are one of their favorite sites to contribute to their city uglification aspirations. Some graffiti "artists" actually think the messes they create enhance the urban environment. The phrase "delusions of grandeur" has never been more apt. To refer to them as a "menace to society" would be a gross understatement. To call these immature brats "artists" would be like calling Tiny Tim a "singer." Sure Tiny Tim opened his mouth and noise came out but the sound he created was so painful to listen to it could only be considered "singing" in the broadest sense of the word.

Perhaps graffiti artists should consider tagging each other's asses and thereby contribute to the uglification of their keisters rather than city neighborhoods. This could provide them with something constructive to do between the hours of 1 o'clock and 4 o'clock in the morning. There has been an ordinance proposed that graffiti purveyors should have to pay for the cost of cleaning up the messes they create in addition to being fined. There is one potential snag to this proposal. Your typical graffiti "artist" does not have two nickels to rub together. You are not likely to locate one in who's who in American society. Trying to find these perpetrators is harder than finding a Republican in San Francisco. What's the sense of finding someone who's next meal will most likely be found in a dumpster or bottom of a garbage can? Do graffiti "artists" ever tag their own property or just someone else's? Of course they don't tag their own property! Who wants to have to clean up the mess they just created? Not taggers! Taggers produce ugliness much more efficiently than they clean it up.

I have seen graffiti in places where Spiderman would be hard pressed to access. Do they suspend themselves on scaffolds for hours at a time in the middle of the night? I suppose where there is a will to defame property there's a way.

Bike Lanes? For Whom?

As the traffic becomes more and more congested I think it's time to evaluate the decision to turn so many of the traffic lanes into bike lanes.

Since San Francisco is one of the hilliest cities in the country, getting from one part of town to another on a bicycle makes absolutely no sense for the vast majority of our citizens. The cross streets near us are Sloat Boulevard and Ocean Avenue. Both streets have had a lane of traffic removed and replaced by a bike lane. You almost never see a bicyclist on either street. Are any of these bike lanes monitored for usage? We need the bike lanes that aren't being used returned to vehicular lanes to ease congestion on our city streets.

It makes no sense for hipster millennial progressives to come along and tell us we no longer need automobiles and that they should be banned from city streets. Their mantra that people can get along just fine using a bicycle and public transportation is just another salvo in San Francisco's "war on families."

Trying to raise a family without the use of an automobile is like trying to write a one-thousand page novel without using the letter "E." Need to go grocery shopping for a family of four at the local store? Why not take the bus, or better yet ride a couple of miles over hill and dale on your trusty Schwinn. Transporting six bags of groceries in your arms while steering the bike should be a "piece of cake." One bag hanging on each handlebar would provide much needed balance. To top it all off (literally) one resting upon your head and you're good to go. As for the purse many women bring along on such occasions, why do you think God gave us teeth?

Need to take a ride to the local mall to buy the kids some new clothes for the coming school year? A quick ten mile bike ride (mostly on the freeway) should bring you to the mall entrance in a few short hours. After enduring this arduous ordeal shopping for clothes would seem like a day at the beach. Getting your shopping bags home would be a snap, unless of course a cloudburst should dampen (literally) your spirits en route. Most likely it wouldn't rain for the entire two hour ride back home. An hour and a half (I would think) at most.

Transporting the youngsters to and from school, after-school activities as well as sports practices and games would simply "take care of itself."

John Lennon famously told us back in 1967 "All You Need Is Love." Perhaps it is time to update this timeless phrase to "All You Need Is a Bicycle."

One of the most significant inventions in the history of humankind isn't going away because a few millennial hipster progressives wish it to be so. The automobile is here to stay. Burying your head in the sand wishing cars would disappear isn't going to change anything. We are long past the point of turning back on cars. They have become an essential part of everyday life for the vast majority of Americans. What we need to do is find ways to power our cars that do not pollute the atmosphere. Whether the source is electricity, solar power or hydrogen fuel cells or perhaps a combination of all three. We can power cars and be eco-friendly at the same time. Automobiles will be around long after hipster millennial progressives are but a dim memory.

Run the Gauntlet

I HAVE A SUGGESTION FOR HEATHER KNIGHT as a followup adventure to her "Total Muni" escapade in which she rode all of the city's bus lines in a single day. Why not embark on a total BART ride in which every BART line is ridden from start to finish for an entire day?

Should she undertake this daunting (and dangerous) challenge an under-garment made of chain-mail could come in handy in the event of a knife attack by some deranged lunatic. A bullet-proof vest would be another option (for obvious reasons). I would also advise making sure her life insurance premiums are paid up (just in case). One can never be too careful regarding life insurance.

Much of this task (it seems to me) would play out like an obstacle course with the challenges varying from one station to the next. At the Powell Street Station (for example) your biggest concern might be stepping around all of the homeless people lying around as far as the eye can see. When the train stopped in the Tenderloin and the doors opened it might be fun to try and count all of the obvious drug addicts and mentally impaired she can spot exiting and entering the train. A downtown stop would be of interest to see how many boarders are already drunk by the early afternoon. Extra points would be awarded for completing any given line without having her purse stolen or getting mugged. Being able to abide the stench of urine and feces would prove invaluable (no gas mask allowed). Another challenge would occur while exiting one station and entering another. The dirt, squalor and filth would prove daunting to even the most battle-hardened commuter. At night (of course) everything seems to be more ominous, foreboding and downright terrifying. This is when the ability to ward off fear (or function in the face of it) can make the difference between soldiering on and tucking one's tail between one's legs and giving up and going home. Being quick and agile can help to avoid being trampled to death by those leaping over the entrance turnstiles as they avoid paying their fare. Should she survive this endless ordeal it might be appropriate to have a t-shirt made up reading "I Ran The BART Gauntlet And Lived To Tell The Tale."

How ironic would it be to survive the BART gauntlet without so much as a scratch only to return to your car and find the windows have been smashed and everything of value has been stolen out of it?

Not on Facebook? Just Who Do You Think You Are?

DEAR BILL AND KAY. IT HAS COME TO OUR attention that the two of you are not on Facebook. What (if anything) are you thinking? For you to shun this most amazing institution borders on insanity. Due to your obstinate refusal to join Facebook and (by extension) the human race no doubt you have noticed a precipitous decline in your popularity amongst friends (should you still have any) and family members. By snubbing Facebook you are turning your back on the vast majority of the human race (such as it is). You are displaying an arrogance that defies comprehension and an attitude that is (quite frankly) toxic. I personally know several lepers whose presence is welcomed considerably more than the two of you.

If you are not on Facebook how are you going to do fun, amazing, awesome, exciting and impressive things, take selfies of yourself doing them, post them on Facebook and make all of your friends insanely jealous because your lives are so much more interesting, exciting, fulfilling, and satisfying than their drab, pointless, boring and pathetic lives. In a nutshell, you can't. If you miss out on this opportunity, you will end up hating yourselves forever (since everyone else already hates you, you may as well make it unanimous).

If not for yourselves, think about your child and grandchild and future generations to come. Do you really want them living with the stigma and embarrassment that would inevitably arise from having progenitors who were not on Facebook? Once the truth got out (as it inevitably would) there would be nothing to stop you from being ostracized, shunned, snubbed, hung in effigy, tarred and feathered, run out of town on a rail and, as a final humiliation, having your library card revoked. Being treated as a social pariah is no "walk in the park" (trust me, I know). Please rethink your refusal to join Facebook. Your very lives may depend on it.

The Relo

All (both) of our loyal readers were amazed by our account of the alien invasion we witnessed recently in the town of Reno, Nevada. We became so enamored with the city and its inhabitants that we have decided to liquidate all of our meager assets and move to this charming hamlet to live out our "golden years" in blissful contentment.

We purchased a vacant warehouse with the intent of refurbishing it and opening a public emporium that caters to the wants and needs of your typical Reno resident. First (and foremost) it will be a gambling casino. It will feature every conceivable way a person can lose money at games of chance. The main draw (of course) will be the endless rows of slot machines. Rather than referring to them as "one arm bandits" (negative connotation) we will call them "payday machines" (positive connotation). This will provide our customers an enhanced sense of their likelihood of actually winning money (which are practically nil).

Here our patrons can happily pull the lever on our "payday machines" while pumping coins into the slots as they puff away on "cancer sticks" (cigarettes) and nursing their favorite "adult beverage." An idyllic scene if ever there was one. Parking will not present a problem for our most loyal customers. "Preferred Parking" spaces will be located nearest to the elevators which whisk you off to the casino so that these losers can start to drop huge sums of money as soon as possible. In fact, our favorite patrons (those who lose the most money) will not have to worry about parking at all. They will be picked up in a chauffeured limousine within a one hundred mile radius and driven straight to the front door. When they are finished losing a king's ransom they will be driven back to their point of origin. Nothing could be more convenient.

Also available for purchase will be every conceivable firearm known to exist. Naturally the ammunition for these most useful implements will also be stocked for (as you know) it is most difficult to kill something (or someone) if one does not possess the requisite ammo. Another crucial aspect of our conglomerate will feature the world's largest tattoo parlour where customers can make themselves even uglier than they were when they arrived (if that's possible). Hideous and extensive tats are de rigueur for so many of Reno's residents.

One of our most popular attractions (no doubt) will be a 500,000 square foot state of the art pawnshop. It is widely known that Reno is a world leader in pawnshop transactions and our store will take full advantage of the many Reno residents who lack ready capitol. It promises to be one of our biggest money makers.

Since our business model is based upon the concept of "one stop shopping" it is crucial to offer a "house of prostitution" within the walls of our warehouse. Any and all forms of sexual perversion will be readily available to our patrons. Customers will have the option of taking advantage of our "senior citizen discount." This does not imply a discount for our elderly guests. Instead our "Johns" will achieve a discount (of up to 75%) if the "lady of the night" they choose for a partner is a senior citizen. The older the "whore" chosen the greater the discount. This is possible because prostitutes "past their prime" do not have to be paid nearly as much as their much younger coworkers.

As a convenience to our clients we will feature an onsite 24 hour pharmacy open to sell various forms of antibiotics, penicillin and various and sundry medications to combat the many virulent forms of venereal diseases that tend to flourish in this type of environment. Alas these medications will have absolutely no effect whatsoever on the maladies our patrons are suffering from but the glimmer of hope they provide are indeed priceless.

Myriad types of jewelry will also be available for purchase at discounts of up to 99% off the suggested retail price. (As you can imagine) a substantial markup will precede the price slashing sales.

Since your typical Reno resident consumes several times the amount of alcohol as the general public at large, all of our bars and cocktail lounges should do a land-office business. As is widely known the sale of alcohol is where the real money lies. What's not to like about a product that is bought at wholesale and then resold to the public after a markup of 8,000 percent?

Prefer to smoke weed, snort cocaine or partake in any other drug of choice? We've got you covered. Any and all forms of narcotics will be kept in stock (for a minimal fee).

Reno residents are keenly aware that a hazy, drunken, drugged out, wasted, totally distorted reality is so much more satisfying, rewarding and fulfilling than actual reality itself. We would be remiss if we did not endeavor to fill a need that more Reno residents have per capita than anywhere in this (or any other) country. That would be along the lines of mental/emotional health issues. Reno is simply awash with schizophrenics, psychotics, hallucinators, people with delusions of grandeur (or squalor) as well as any other mental affliction known to man. For this reason we will have a team of quacks (I.E. shyster "medical experts") on hand to analyze and treat any episode that may arise. Though none of those involved in these treatments will actually be real doctors, several of them have played one on TV. Our stated goal for every crisis that arises is for our shamans (or witch-doctors) to not make the situation much worse than it was when the patient arrived. Though this lofty aspiration is not always (if ever) attainable it gives our faux M.D.'s something to shoot for.

Since so many Reno residents are hell-bent on so many forms of depravity we endeavor to provide them with the opportunity to feed their loathsome and despicable habits.

"Breathing While Black"

THERE HAS BEEN A LOT OF TALK RECENTLY about the "Black Lives Matter" movement, police brutality against African Americans and why so many Blacks are being killed by police officers even though they are unarmed and pose no threat to said policemen. This has become a chronic and persistent problem and the underlying causes must be addressed.

It would be easy to ascribe guilt in these tragedies to racist, bigoted, brutal, uncaring maniacs who have no concern for human life and are disguised as police officers. This would be seeing the problem in an oversimplified context that could miss the root causes of their actions. After all, they don't call them "peace officers" for nothing (or do they?).

It is widely known that in order to instill a peaceful environment occasionally a perfectly innocent Black person's life will have to be sacrificed "for the common good." This is assumed as inevitable among most policemen and the technical term most officers prefer is "collateral damage."

A recent study of Blacks killed by policemen clearly indicates that virtually all of the victims were, during these lethal confrontations, committing the unpardonable sin of "breathing while Black." B.W.B. is now against the law in most southern states (and the District of Columbia). Though originally considered a misdemeanor the seriousness of this infraction has caused it to be reclassified (in most cases) as a felony. It has been proven, beyond the shadow of a doubt, that in virtually every case of "innocent" Blacks dying at the hands of an "officer of the law" they were brazenly "breathing while Black" (until they weren't).

It is time we looked at another aspect of this controversial issue. It is widely known that policemen (and women) are not the best educated of our citizenry. Far from it. Most possess a perfunctory education at best. Detailed knowledge of biology, the respiratory system and the vital role the lungs and the pulmonary artery play in human health is far beyond the ken of your typical cop. These subjects are commonly part of a college curriculum. When (I ask you) is the last time you encountered a police officer who had graduated from college? Neither have I.

I am confident that we have established most (if not all) "peace officers" are simply clueless as to the crucial role breathing plays in our very existence. Breathing is a complex process that is not fully understood by even the brightest of nitwits. To expect a policeman to grasp the subtle nuances involved in breathing in and breathing out is asking way too much of these simple-minded buffoons.

Please understand I am not trying to rationalize or condone these senseless killings or (to use the technical term) murders, I am simply trying to shine a light on possible explanations for the behavior of people who view themselves as judge, jury, and executioner all wrapped in one murderous package.

If they are completely ignorant of the vital role breathing plays in our life, liberty and the pursuit of living for another day, can you really blame a police officer when they hear a Black scream at the top of his lungs "I can't breathe" for thinking "and your point is?"

Dr. Einstein tells us that everything is relative. There is an old saying that goes "time flies while you're having fun." If this is true (and I believe it is) then the opposite must also be true. I make this point to show that if someone has their knee pressed against your neck for 9 minutes it can seem like an eternity (not having fun). However if you are a police officer who enjoys cutting off the air supply of a prone helpless Black person those same nine minutes can literally fly by. It all depends on whether you are being choked to death, or the one doing the choking.

Cease Jogging At a Red Light? Not on Your Life

HAVE YOU EVER BEEN WALKING ALONG A CITY street and had to stop because of a red light? I thought so. Perhaps you have had a jogger come up from behind and had to also stop because of the red light. If so you no doubt noticed one thing. The jogger never stops jogging and just stand there for the five or ten seconds it takes for the light to turn green. Apparently that would be bad. The jogger continues to jog in place for however long it takes for the light to change. What the hell is going on here? Exactly what does the joggers suppose would happen to them if they actually stopped moving for a few seconds? Do they think they might self-immolate? Spontaneously combust? Suffer a deadly, lethal, mortal, fatal cramp over their entire body?

Maybe they envision themselves melting into nothingness suffering the same fate as the Wicked Witch of the West did when Dorothy accidentally doused her with a bucket of water. If so I have a newsflash for these exercise freaks. You can stop jogging for a few seconds and survive. There has been documentation by reliable sources of joggers (on more than one occasion) brazenly stopping at a light without continuing to jog and living to tell the tale. The courage, bravery and just plain guts displayed by these thrill-seeking daredevils is truly admirable. To risk life and limb while ignoring the distinct possibility of suffering an excruciatingly painful death speaks of a "throw caution to the wind" attitude that few of us possess. Ceasing to jog while stopped at a red light is considered (by most experts) to be every bit as dangerous as "taking candy from a baby" and perhaps just as difficult. So if you have a death wish (or know someone who does) try jogging in the city and when you happen upon a light that is red stop moving altogether (if you dare). Should you survive you've got a tale worth telling your grandchildren about though they may find it difficult to believe such an unlikely story.

OMG Congress Finally Makes Lynching a Hate Crime - Who Knew?

CONGRESS GAVE THE FINAL APPROVAL THIS week to legislation that for the first time would make lynching a hate crime in the U.S. This begs an obvious question. What was it before? It took until the year 2022 to declare lynching a hate crime? "The wheels of justice turn slowly" has never been defined in a better fashion. 200 bills have been introduced over the past century that have tried to ban lynching in America but until the Emmett Till Antilynching Act was approved by Congress they all had failed. It took 201 attempts to outlaw lynching? So you think someone is smart just because they are in Congress? Think again. They are in Congress because they won an election not because they think lynching is a crime. The act is named for Emmett Till, a Black teenager who made the unfortunate decision to whistle at a White girl which resulted in his being brutally lynched in Mississippi in 1955.

The House overwhelmingly approved a similar measure in 2020 but it was blocked by the Senate. Blocked by the Senate in 2020? Did they suppose the time just wasn't right to outlaw lynching? Perhaps they feared offending southern White bigoted, racist, intolerant, hate-filled maniacs whose IQ's are lower than the winter temperature in West Yellowstone, Wyoming (at night). This (to me) is perfectly understandable. After all, southern White bigoted, racist, intolerant, hate-filled maniacs are (I'm sure you'll agree) the last people you want to offend.

The word lynch probably originated from Charles Lynch a Virginia painter in the 1700's who, along with his neighbors took the law into their own hands in punishing Tories (British sympathizers) who plundered their property. Throughout the south it became a time honored tradition and soon fathers would pass on the skills necessary to lynch effectively much the same as so many fathers pass along the tradition of baseball or fishing to their young sons. In much of the south even today hunting (Black people) for fun and sport remains one of the more popular pastimes below the Mason-Dixon line.

It would be impossible to broach the subject of lynching without mentioning the most vile, heinous, evil, dastardly and treacherous organization to have existed in the history of humankind. I speak of (as you have no doubt surmised) the Ku Klux Klan. Led by their "Grand Wizard" the clan was noted for their hatred of Catholics and Jews but it was their desire to exterminate the Black race altogether that inspired them to transition from burning crosses on people's lawns to hanging Black people from the nearest tree. The KKK did not invent lynching. They simply perfected, popularized and took wonton murder to a whole new level. The obsessive focus on lynching Blacks in the most efficient manner possible serves to reinforce the clan motto that if lynching is worth doing at all it is worth doing well. If there is one thing these robed, white sheeted (their horses too) pointy-headed, torch-carrying monstrosities possess it is the desire to do their job as thoroughly as possible. Hopefully if the Emmett Till Antilynching Act puts a lot of KKK members out of a job they may find work in a related field. Perhaps the mafia could use some hitmen and are hiring people with years or even decades of experience murdering people without any justification.

Part II
Life in "Baghdad By the Bay" in the 21st Century

By Kenneth Jones

Regarding "Children Becoming Increasingly Rare"

Congratulations to the powers that be in San Francisco. They appear to be winning decisively in their "War on Families." The percentage of the population in San Francisco under the age of 18 fell to 13% in the 2020 census San Francisco remains the most childless city in the entire country. We're number one! Makes a body proud. You can try and blame the high cost of living but cities such as Honolulu and New York, which are equally expensive, are both at 21% of the population being under 18.

What happened to the San Francisco of the 50's and 60's when families with children could be found on every residential block in the city?

Millennials, hipsters and progressives tell us all we need to live in San Francisco is a bicycle and public transportation. Ever try raising a family without the benefit of an automobile? I didn't think so. But good luck with that if you do.

We have teachers who are living in someone's basement because they can't afford the rent on a studio apartment. Why bother paying teachers a livable wage when 87% of San Franciscans are not of school age? If current trends continue we will soon have more homeless people in San Francisco than children. This could be a good thing since in San Francisco there is much more concern, compassion and money for the homeless (350 millions dollars a year) than for our children. But why dwell on the negative. Sure there are only 115,000 children living in the city. But we have 150,000 dogs!

Chesa Boudin Needs to Get His Head Out of His Ass and Do His Job

THE TRAGIC DEATH OF 7 MONTH OLD SYNCIERE Williams is the latest example of Chesa Boudin's failure to do his job.

Joseph Williams was booked by police for allegedly murdering the child. He had been arrested twice recently on suspicion of felony domestic violence before being released without charges.

As he has done in the past Boudin shifted the blame to the victim for refusing to cooperate with prosecutors. However, Kathy Black, director of Casa de las Madres shelter pointed out "Domestic violence is a crime against the state of California and it's the district attorney's job to develop the evidence to prevent a case and not the victims." Perhaps Chesa Boudin is not fully aware of just what his job entails.

In the last three months of 2020 city cops made 131 arrests for felony domestic violence and Boudin's office dismissed 113 of them. No batterers program, no anger management classes, no required supervision for visiting children.

When Beverly Upton, director of the San Francisco Domestic Violence Consortium participated in two zoom meetings with Boudin she was startled to hear the district attorney repeatedly talk about the need to unclog the court system of domestic violence cases. Is it any wonder that domestic violence victims feel ignored and marginalized in San Francisco?

Once again Chesa Boudin and the district attorney's office's failure to do its job has led directly to the death of two more people in San Francisco, this time in the Potrero Hill neighborhood. Saturday's back to back fatal shootings of 61 year old Darryl Haynes and 54 year old Randy Armstrong were allegedly perpetrated by 32 year old San Francisco resident Robert Newt. During a search of his vehicle police found an unserialized and untraceable AR-15 style firearm. Newt was taken into custody and booked on multiple charges including possession of a firearm, discharging a firearm in a grossly negligent manner and driving without a license.

Incredibly Newt was released from jail after the D.A.'s office declined to file charges. Apparently district attorney Boudin didn't want to spoil Mr. Newt's day by charging him with crimes and keeping him incarcerated. Back out on the street Mr. Newt predictably went on a crime spree that resulted in two deaths. How smart do you have to be to realize that Robert Newt represented a clear and present danger to the citizenry of San Francisco? A lot smarter than Chesa Boudin it would seem.

Chesa Boudin

So the Chesa Boudin era in San Francisco has begun. With his decision to withdraw criminal charges against a man who attacked police officers with a bottle he has confirmed concerns he would be soft on crime and more sympathetic towards criminals than police officers and victims.

The city's police union accused Boudin of giving a "green light" to criminals to attack police. Jamaica Hampton was originally charged with assault with a deadly weapon, assault upon a police officer and threats to an officer. Ed Obayashi, a Plumas County sheriff's deputy and instructor on use-of-force investigations called Boudin's decision "irresponsible." San Jose police chief Eddie Garcia called Boudin's decision "Shocking and despicable." "I feel terrible for the courageous men and women of the S.F.P.D." He added is it any wonder the police officers association vehemently opposed Boudin's election?

In the latest example of Chesa Boudin's inept incompetence two pedestrians were killed in downtown San Francisco by Troy Ramon McAlister, a parolee who remained free despite being arrested several times in the city in recent months. McAlister was intoxicated and driving a stolen car. Though Mr. McAlister was released on April 10th from a state prison sentence for robbery, he was not charged with any new crimes by the district attorney's office.

San Francisco police chief Bill Scott called the deaths "A senseless tragedy that should not have happened." Mr. Boudin tried to shift the blame for the deaths to state parole officers for not holding McAlister for a single day following his

Dec. 20th arrest. Boudin later acknowledged "Clearly it was a mistake to think parole supervision would be adequate." No doubt Mr. Boudin's 20/20 hindsight will be a great comfort to the grieving families.

According to Rockne Harmon, a retired Alameda County senior deputy district attorney "It is not parole officer's responsibility to make charging decisions." Is there anyone else you'd like to try and blame Mr. Boudin?

It would appear that wearing an ankle monitor does not prevent a serial criminal from continuing to commit crimes. Who knew? Not Chesa Boudin. Perhaps Mr. Boudin thought an ankle monitor would magically transform Erlin Romero into a model citizen. Alas, it did not happen.

In the latest example of district attorney Chesa Boudin releasing a criminal from incarceration only to have him commit more crimes, Mr. Romero is now charged with two counts of kidnapping, first degree robbery and car theft. Romero was already facing two open cases for robbery and car theft out of San Francisco when he was released from jail.

Supervisor Catherine Stefani said the abduction was the latest example of a city that is "out of control with crimes being committed by people who were previously arrested and not held in jail." "On top of the horrifying kidnapping we've seen two women killed on New Years Eve, a young father killed in an eight-vehicle crash and a fatal midday attack on our seniors." "We cannot keep releasing dangerous individuals back on the street after arrests only to see them commit more crimes." How will Chesa Boudin deal with Erlin Romero now? Two ankle monitors?

"San Francisco is and will continue to be a safe city" said district attorney Chesa Boudin. I wonder which of the 39 cities of the world named San Francisco Mr. Boudin is referring to because it certainly can't be the one in California. Or perhaps he is experiencing the first stage of grief because he is definitely in denial about the safety of San Francisco's citizens. The deaths of Jack Palladino and Vicha Ratanapakdee are just the latest examples of gun violence and residential and commercial break-ins in the city.

There were 48 killings in San Francisco in 2020 up from 41 a year ago. The number of recorded shots fired in the first seven months of 2020 rose 32 percent over the same period in 2019. Burglaries rose 47 percent in 2020 compared with the prior year.

Instead of denying there is a safety problem in the city and shifting the blame when he is criticized he needs to keep violent criminals behind bars and stop releasing them back on to the street so they can continue to ply their chosen trade. Haters are gonna hate. Criminals are gonna commit crimes. It's not rocket science.

There is one aspect of the job of district attorney that Chesa Boudin has demonstrated total mastery of since assuming office. Mr. Boudin has displayed extraordinary tact and comfort in offering his condolences to the families of murder victims who were killed by people who should have been behind bars. Of course he's had a lot of practice and as they say "Practice makes perfect."

Should he ever tire of offering condolences to grieving families maybe he will start doing the job he was elected to do. Charge violent criminals with the crimes they have committed so they can be tried, convicted and removed from society. San Francisco needs a district attorney who doesn't think that slapping the wrist of a violent criminal constitutes "cruel and unusual punishment."

A Dog's Life

If you were to walk around downtown San Francisco for any length of time you would be sure to notice certain things. One (no doubt) would be the proliferation of homeless people littering the sidewalks, doorways and alleys of our city.

There are a couple of things that amaze me about so many of our homeless citizens. No matter what time of day or night I encounter these people so many of them are lying on the ground covered in blankets appearing to be asleep. My question is just what is it they do that makes them so tired that they require so much rest? When is the last time you saw a homeless person participating in a marathon (or even a half marathon, for that matter)? The homeless are seldom (if ever) spotted at the local 24 Hour Fitness working up a sweat exercising. Since the vast majority of the homeless are unemployed it is highly unlikely they reached a state of exhaustion from putting in a hard day's work. Those that aren't sleeping are sitting down holding a sign begging for money because they don't have any and you do.

It simply amazes me as I walk around the city how many homeless people have a dog. They are sitting or lying on the sidewalk with their dogs who are sitting or lying on the sidewalk with them. Since most dogs require frequent exercise to stay in optimal health I can't help thinking that these dogs are living (quite literally) a dog's life. Shouldn't it be required of a dog owner to be able to take care of themselves before they can take care of a dog? What kind of a home can a person who has no home provide for a dog? I would assume that the food the homeless procure for their animal does not meet the nutritional value required to maintain a healthy dog. Where are the animal control officers? Get these poor dogs away from the homeless and into a home. I'm tired of seeing dogs sitting on a street corner knowing that is all the dog is going to do all day (and night).

I sometimes wonder why you almost always see the homeless with a dog but never with a cat. Your typical cat is a finicky eater and will not consume just anything tossed at it. If you try to boss around a cat it's likely to respond by ignoring its tormenter, hissing and baring its claws or turning its back and walking away. Cats abhor the smell of urine and waste matter eliminated from the bowels (excrement). Dogs, however, often go out of their way to smell the vilest of odors so that the foulest emination wafting from a homeless encampment does not phase them in the least. The homeless have no use for cats and cats have even less use for the homeless.

Call It Christmas

THANK YOU FOR THE ARTICLE BY BOB GARDner "Just Call It Christmas." "Get over it folks."

It's about time someone fired a salvo against the "War on Christmas." For some inexplicable reason in ultra politically correct San Francisco it has become a faux pas to so much as mention the word Christmas. Apparently there are a growing number of people who are offended by the term. For what reason I have no idea. Perhaps they are bothered by the fact that Christians seem to enjoy celebrating the birth of the man who founded the world's most popular religion. Since Jesus is arguably the most significant and influential person ever to have lived I find this attitude curious.

These people's attempts to avoid Christmas is manifested by sending out "Mock Christmas Cards" that are totally bereft of depictions of traditional Christmas scenes or sentiments. The phrase "Merry Christmas" has been replaced with the generic "Seasons Greetings" or "Happy Holidays."

My wife, who taught in the S.F.U.S.D. for decades described to me how they no longer celebrate Christmas at school (lest they offend someone). No more (fireproof) Christmas tree, no more singing Christmas carols, no more Christmas play. No more Santa coming to school and passing out candy canes. No more classroom Christmas party. An assembly to celebrate Kwanzaa or Lunar New Year is fine, but not Christmas. It would seem that Kwanzaa and Lunar New Year are politically correct but Christmas is not. Scrooge (no doubt) would be pleased.

Mick LaSalle Knows Nothing About Pop Music

ARGUABLY THE BEST ADVICE A WRITER CAN receive is "Write what you know." When Mick LaSalle writes about the cinema he does just that. When he writes about pop music he does not. His statement in last Sunday's pink section that "You can take all the pop music released in the U.S. from Jan. 1st, 1960 through Kennedy's assassination in November 1963 and throw it in the dumpster" exposes an ignorance of the music scene during this time period that is (to put it bluntly) appalling. The fact that he also tries to argue that the 70's was a more prolific decade for pop music than the 60's clearly demonstrates his knowledge of pop music is practically nil.

To disparage all of the great artists and their music that gave those of us who had their ears glued to the radio during those years so much pleasure and enjoyment serves to underscore the fact that Mr. Lasalle's appreciation of early 60's pop music is woefully inadequate.

In an effort to educate Mr. LaSalle as to the quality of the music that was on the airwaves during those years I have compiled a list of the artists whose songs and albums were on the charts from January 1960 through December 1963. Paul Anka, Joan Baez, Hank Ballard, The Beach Boys, Tony Bennet, Brook Benton and Dinah Washington, Gary U.S. Bonds, Booker T. and the M.G.'s, Pat Boone, James Brown, Dave Brubeck, Johnny Burnette, Jerry Butler, Freddie Cannon, Johnny

Cash, Ray Charles, Chubby Checker, Patsy Cline, Nat "King" Cole, Sam Cooke, The Crystals, Bobby Darin, Dion, Fats Domino, The Drifters, Bob Dylan, The Everly Brothers, The Four Seasons, Connie Francis, Marvin Gaye, Leslie Gore, The Impressions, The Isley Brothers, Ben E. King, Brenda Lee, Barbara Lewis, Martha and the Vandellas, Clyde McPhatter, The Miracles, Rickey Nelson, Roy Orbison, Peter, Paul and Mary, Gene Pitney, Elvis Presley, Bobby Rydell, Neil Sedaka, The Shirelles, The Tokens, Lenny Welch, Andy Williams, Jackie Wilson and Stevie Wonder. No fewer than 30 of these artists or groups have been enshrined in the Rock and Roll Hall of Fame. Apparently Mr. LaSalle was not consulted as to their qualifications for induction. Possibly Mr. LaSalle should stick to reviewing movies and leave critiquing pop music to those who know what they are talking about. As Abraham Lincoln was quoted as saying "It is better to keep your mouth closed and be thought ignorant than to open it and remove all doubt." Mick LaSalle opened his mouth.

Ranked Choice Voting
Partly Responsible

It would be easy to blame Chesa Boudin for the deaths of Elizabeth Platt and Hanako Abe. Boudin had passed on several opportunities to charge suspect Troy Ramon McAlister with crimes he committed but chose to refer the incidents to state parole officers instead. Mr. McAlister is a career criminal who has been in trouble with the law his entire adult life and the district attorney repeatedly put him back on the street to continue his crime spree.

To my mind another factor was crucial in the deaths of two innocent victims. Were it not for the failed and flawed system of ranked choice voting Chesa Boudin would have never been elected in the first place. At the time of the election political analyst David Latterman said Chesa Boudin had "Zero chance" of beating Suzy Loftus in a run-off election. Had a more moderate candidate won the election there is an excellent chance Troy Ramon McAlister would have been behind bars where he belonged. Instead we have a district attorney who shows more compassion and sympathy for the perpetrators of crimes than he does for the victims.

Elvis Not on Rock and Roll's Mt. Rushmore? OMG

Dear Mick LaSalle,

Elvis Presely not on the Mt. Rushmore of Rock and Roll? He was great for only two years tops? Really? Who knew? In the book "The Billboard Book of Top 40 Hits" Joel Whitburn devised a point system to rank the most popular artists and groups that graced the pop charts from 1955 through 1987. The point system is based on an artist or group's song's highest charted position and the total weeks each song was on the charts. Using this system, during the first three decades of the pop/rock era The Beatles came in second with 2,975 points. Elvis Presley had 5,131. There is as great a difference in point totals between Elvis Presley and The Beatles as there is between The Beatles at No. 2 and artist No. 74 (Tom Jones). Under the category of most charted records The Beatles were again second with 49. Elvis had 107. For the most top 10 records Elvis is first with 38. The most weeks with a song in the number one position we have Elvis with 80 and The Beatles once again in second with 59. Broken up into decades Elvis was number one in the 1950's, No. 2 (just behind The Beatles) in the 1960's and as late as the 1970's he was in the number 13 slot right behind the Eagles. You opened your mouth again Mr. LaSalle.

I can hardly wait for your next proclamation regarding your knowledge of pop music. Perhaps you will inform us that James Brown and Aretha Franklin do not belong on soul music's Mt. Rushmore because they were only great for "two years, tops."

Regarding Overdoses Caused 699 Deaths in San Francisco in 2020

THREE TIMES AS MANY PEOPLE DIED IN SAN Francisco last year from drug overdoses than from Covid-19. In addition Narcan, a lifesaving overdose reversal drug was administered at least 3,400 times up from 2,610 times in 2019. Kristan Marshall, the director of the drug overdose and prevention and education project tells us the root problem of these overdose deaths is homelessness, poverty and racism. Is it really a logical consequence of being homeless, living in poverty or being subjected to racism to become a drug addict? If I had no home to live in, no money or was being discriminated against I doubt if I would acerbate my problems by becoming addicted to drugs.

Often we hear about people who have "fallen through the cracks," "been neglected by society," "made bad decisions," have "fallen in with the wrong crowd" or are suffering from "substance abuse addiction." Somehow their will to make positive lifestyle choices has been taken away from them. In San Francisco we feel the need to make excuses for people's shortcomings and make them out to be victims. Is it ever the fault of the addict for a lack of character, self-control and self-discipline and selfishly thinking only of oneself? Whatever happened to taking responsibility and being accountable for one's failures. People need to own the choices they make. I'm sick of lame excuses and idiotic platitudes. Wake up and join the human race.

Just Wondering

THERE HAS BEEN A LOT OF CONTROVERSY OVER who is worthy of having his or her name on a public school, street or building. Apparently a "Morals Police" has been formed to determine whose character, ethics, honesty, moral principle as well as a strong sense of compassion and what is right and wrong would justify their name being considered for such an honor. Amazingly some of the names being considered to be dropped include those of Washington, Lincoln and Jefferson. It seems they did not "pass inspection." Would it be safe to assume the name Donald J. Trump will not be recommended for consideration for the foreseeable future?

S.F. Pay

If San Francisco Director of Health Dr. Grant Colfax is ever asked how he feels about making more money ($475,612) than the president of the United States ($400,000). I have a suggestion for his reply. He should say exactly what Babe Ruth said in the 1920's when asked the same question. Why not? I had a better year than he did.

Rename Board of Ed

RATHER THAN GOING TO ALL THE TROUBLE AND expense of renaming 44 San Francisco schools, why don't we just rename the Board of Education instead? "The Inquisition?" Sounds appropriate.

Regarding Teen Suspect in S.F. Killing to be Tried in Sacramento

I APPLAUD THE DECISION TO PROSECUTE THE 17 year old boy accused of murder during a sideshow in The Excelsior. The last thing we need is to give Chesa Boudin another opportunity to give a violent criminal a slap on the wrist and put him back on the street as soon as possible.

Sacramento prosecutors are petitioning a judge to have the 17 year old tried in an adult court. How can it be that someone who is one day shy of their 18th birthday at the time a crime is committed is not responsible for their action but if he or she is one day older they are? The 18 year old cut-off is totally arbitrary. The decision to try a perpetrator as an adult should be based on age, the seriousness of the crime and if it involves a repeat offender. Each case should be judged individually rather than a one-size-fits-all policy. Over the past two years Sacramento prosecutors filed nearly 2,500 cases in juvenile court and sought to transfer a minor to adult court in about 1% of them. The boy, who is from Sacramento was already in custody there facing two counts of attempted murder with gang enhancement. Just how old does one need to be to understand the commandment "Thou shalt not kill"?

S.F.'s Response to Drug Epidemic?
Make It Easier to Acquire Drugs

SENATOR SCOTT WEINER PLANS TO REINTRO-
duce legislation that would allow "safe drug use sites" in San Francisco and
Oakland. How does allowing addicts to inject drugs (gratis) encourage them
to get into treatment and overcome their habit? It is now widely known among
health experts that the best way to get someone to stop indulging in negative
behavior is to simply allow them the opportunity to continue this behavior
(gratis) in a supervised and safe environment. Allowing drug addicts to consume
and feed their habit will (no doubt) have them off of drugs virtually overnight.
By sending them the message it's OK to shoot up as long as they are safe and
supervised they soon see the folly of their ways and most will never so much as
touch a drug again. Why this brilliant technique was not employed centuries ago
I'm sure I have no idea. If ingesting their preferred drug becomes too easy all the
challenge to drug taking has been removed and the fun completely vanishes. After
one or two sessions in a safe-injection site many addicts have forgotten why the
hell they ever took drugs in the first place. Problem solved.

I know there are those of you who will have doubts that providing addicts
with drugs (gratis) will do nothing to help them kick the drug habit and is in
reality counter-intuitive. Recent studies indicate, however, that intuition is not
what it is cracked up to be (and never was). Besides smarter people than you or I
are backing this proposal (I.E. Scott Weiner) so it must have merit. The reason

I know that Scott Weiner is smarter than you and I is that Mr. Weiner is a state senator and you and I are not. State senators are always much smarter than their constituents. That's why they are state senators. Wait a minute. Isn't Scott Weiner the same Scott Weiner who keeps proposing a bill to extend the drinking hours in San Francisco from 2 a.m. to 4 a.m.? And it keeps getting voted down? Mr. Weiner shrewdly surmises that San Franciscans can't possibly achieve the desired level of inebriation by 2 o'clock in the morning and an extra two hours of alcohol consumption is what this city needs. Mr. Weiner is simply a master of counter-intuition.

One thing that amazes me is why hasn't Senator Weiner proposed safe alcohol consumption sites where those who are addicted to alcohol can be provided with free alcohol in a safe and supervised environment. Alcoholics should have the same opportunity as drug addicts to continue their dependence on their drug of choice. Why should alcoholics have to pay to get drunk when addicts can abuse drugs for free? A.S.A.C.S. could provide companionship for alcoholics who don't like drinking alone (lets face it, who does?). Paramedics would be on hand ready to respond to the first sign of alcohol poisoning ready to administer life-saving techniques. Unarguably a win-win situation.

In the spirit of San Francisco inclusiveness I would like to suggest "free grazing sights" where obest overeaters addicted to food could feed their faces and gorge themselves to their heart's content on all the food (gratis) they desire. Only three visits a day would be permissible but each visit could last several hours. Medics would be monitoring the entire operation and could (in a moment's notice) be ready to spring into action to apply the heimlich maneuver in case an over avid feaster was choking on a chicken bone.

By allowing addicts to embrace their addiction you have taken the first step towards total recovery. Right?

Safe Haven for Drugs

So it has finally come to this in San Francisco. Even liberal democratic former mayor Gavin Newsom says that San Francisco is too lax on disgraceful street life and has become too permissive toward open drug use and other behavior on the city's streets. "You can be too permissive and I happen to think we have crossed that threshold in this state," Newsom said "you see it." "It's just disgraceful."

In the same issue of the Chronicle Heather Knight called San Francisco a "safe haven for drug dealers." Police say drug dealers from the East Bay ride BART into San Francisco every day to sell to San Francisco's addicts. "In San Francisco," she goes on, "It is easier to buy heroin, meth and crack than to obtain a liquor license for a new restaurant." Drug dealers are often arrested multiple times in one year but the courts regularly release the suspects while their cases are pending. No consequences and no accountability. If you were a drug dealer or abuser where else would you want to be? Lax courts. "Soft on crime" judges. Permissive culture and sensibilities.

San Francisco is just like a spoiled brat of a child whose new-age parents decided they did not want their kid to hear the word "no." This (to me) is a curious attitude for a parent to have since "no" is the most important word for a child to learn and understand. It teaches a child there are some things you can do and some things you can't do (what a concept!). Limits, self discipline, self control, and understanding authority all begin with knowing exactly what the word no means.

Without it the child sees it can do whatever it wants with no fear of punishment or repercussions. You now have an out-of-control child that will not listen to or obey adult authority. The child now simply does whatever it feels like doing like the drug dealers and users in San Francisco.

Who Wants to Stop? No One

ADVOCATES OF THE "IDAHO STOP" LAW TELL US it is safe for cyclists to roll through an intersection and coast through a stop sign or light if no traffic is approaching. Most cyclists I have observed do not even bother to slow down. If the "Idaho Stop" is safe for people on a bicycle it is also safe for people inside an automobile. How many times have you had to stop at a stop sign or red light with no traffic to be seen in any direction. If traffic signs can be ignored by cyclists why can't they be ignored by motorists? People in a car are encased in a protective shell often with airbags on the inside of the doors. Someone on a bicycle has a plastic helmet on their head. It is amazing how bullit-proof so many cyclists imagine themselves to be judging from the way they fly around town with reckless abandon. Perhaps they think they are safer on their bicycle with a piece of plastic on their heads than someone in 2,000 pounds of steel. If so I have some bad news for them should they collide with a car. Or maybe they think your typical motorist is so kind, compassionate and understanding of how vulnerable cyclists are on their bicycles. Again, more bad news. Motorists are keenly aware that if a collision occurs between their car and someone on a bicycle it is the cyclist who will end up in the morgue and not the motorist. Why they behave like the opposite is true I have no idea. Stupidity? Delusions of grandeur? A false sense of security? A death wish? A desire to appear in the newspaper or on the ten o'clock news? Or perhaps a combination of all of the above. Cyclists do not want to have to stop at stop signs or red lights when it is safe to proceed. Guess what, neither do motorists.

Immigration Problem - Solved

WITH ALL THE TALK OF THE IMMIGRATION problems I'm surprised the simplest solution is never mentioned or proposed. The countries that send the most immigrants to America are China, Mexico, India and the Philippines. What is it that makes these countries places that so many people want to escape from rather than live in? The wages paid to your typical worker and the overall standard of living are so low it's a wonder so many of them ever reach adulthood. Then there is the graft, bribery and corruption that is rampant in all levels of government. High crime rates, poor health care and sanitation standards (quite literally in the toilet) as well as inferior education opportunities also add to the problems. Often they come here seeking relief from political, religious or racial persecution. Many come to our country for the opportunity to attend colleges and universities in the United States to further their educations.

Others fear for their lives due to out-of-control lawlessness and gang violence. Drug cartels are responsible for indiscriminate killing in many parts of Mexico making certain areas resemble a war zone more than a place to live. There are more violent deaths in El Salvador than any country but Syria. How did these countries become places people want to escape from rather than live in? As the Stylistics told us back in the day "People make the world go round." People are also the cause of all these problems faced by so many of the world's nations. As usual it starts right at the top. Too often the leaders of these countries, government

& officials, politicians and everyone with an iota of power are in it only for their own benefit. Far too many of these people simply want to line their own pockets with ill gotten wealth. These countries are literally bereft of a middle class. You have the extremely wealthy at the top and the 99 percenters at the bottom. To put it bluntly the "swamp needs to be drained." Corruption, kickbacks, bribes, shady deals, graft and a rigged political system must end. Standards need to be raised across the board and people need to be elected or hired who aren't in it for only themselves. Too many countries of the world are of the third variety (don't get me started on Africa) where migrants are fleeing in droves trying to gain access to Europe. If these counties can be transformed into places people actually want to live in, the immigration problem will be a thing of the past.

"Oxford town, Oxford tow

OK Not OK

It would seem the ridiculousness of the modern world knows no limitations. If you want to find a city that can compete with San Francisco in being uber politically correct, progressive and is all about no one being offended there is only one place to go. That would be Berkeley. Where else?

Only in Berkeley can you even approach the level of idiocy and new-age sensibilities. Back in the day Berkeley was a hot-bed for anti Vietnam war protests, free speech rallies, political activism, sit-ins, be-ins, civil rights marches, save the whale (and every other endangered species) petitions to be signed and every other left wing organizing you could possibly think of. More bras were burned (per capita) in Berkeley than anywhere on Earth. The city leans so far to the left it is in danger of falling into San Francisco bay. Organic food is omnipresent and clinics are everywhere you look. Acupuncture, herbal medicines and holistic healing are more popular than actual doctors. If you yearn for the 60's and the hippie culture that flourished go to Berkeley and you will be immersed in that very atmosphere. Environmental issues and the ecology are issues of great interest in Berkeley. There have even been documented instances of people being tarred, feathered dand run out of town on a rail for littering (and deservedly so I might add).

It is no wonder that in this city the Jewish Anti-Defamation League has added the age-old OK hand gesture to its list of hate symbols. It seems that making a circle with one's thumb and forefinger with three other digits upraised qualifies as a gesture of hate. It is comforting to know that San Francisco's board of supervisors aren't the only ones who have so much time on their hands they can afford to waste it making pointless, absurd and inane edicts and proclamations.

I can scarcely imagine how many hours of scholarly research that was required to determine that the people flashing the OK sign were in reality blatantly perpetuating a culture of hate unbeknownst to the less astute amongst us. I suppose I should have known all along that the OK sign was actually a thinly veiled act of racism, bias and hate. In retrospect had I possessed keener wits it would have been as clear as mud. Once again we have found that if you look hard enough for something you are sure to find it.

Fees At S.F. General

I don't see what is so remarkable about the exorbitant fees being charged for care received at San Francisco General Hospital. These rates are apparently agreed upon by the board of supervisors and the mayor. According to Heather Knight they include $29,924 for setting foot in the hospital with a major trauma. Nina Dang broke her arm in a bicycle accident and was charged $24,074.50. Couldn't they have, at least, given her a pass on the fifty cents?

You might not want to go to S.F. General if you are suffering from a migraine. Alicia Ridriguez did and now owes the hospital more than $10,000. I can't help wondering if the arrival of that bill caused a relapse of her headache.

Are these outrageous charges really so surprising in a city where a modest two bedroom two bath house can fetch upwards of 1 ½ million dollars? Or a one bedroom apartment can cost you 2 thousand dollars a month? To rent?

Once again the rest of the nation is laughing their collective asses off at what is considered fair and equitable in the city of San Francisco.

Elon Musk's Flamethrower

HAS ELON MUSK TAKEN LEAVE OF HIS SENSES? Perhaps he is off his rocker looking for the marbles he lost. At the very least he is living proof one can become extremely wealthy without the benefit of as much common sense as your typical four year old.

All indications point to the fact that there are more and more people out there who are immature, senseless and make idiotic decisions on a regular basis. Into this climate Elcon Musk wants to market a flamethrower? To what purpose? What good could possibly come from every dim-witted moron with half a brain and the means to buy a flamethrower having the opportunity to purchase one. Mr. Musk was quoted as saying "I know it's a little off brand, but kids love it." So he's marketing flamethrowers to children? Parents all over the country must be jumping for joy. No need to fret over what to get Johnny for his fifth birthday. A flamethrower would fit the bill perfectly. If Johnny's little sister is particularly annoying a judiciously employed flamethrower should put an end to that problem posthaste. He goes on to say what a good investment his flamethrower would be because of the impending zombie apocalypse. It would seem that the apocalypse has already begun and Mr. Musk is the presiding zombie-in-chief. Zombies are usually thought to be the walking dead. It has become clear that Mr. Musk is a chartered member of the walking brain-dead.

In addition to the physical mayhem that will inevitably ensue, how many wildfires will result from the misuse of the Musk flamethrower? Another Napa inferno perhaps? In what might be the most amazing aspect of all (I am not making this up) a bill that would require warning labels on the flamethrower stalled in the assembly appropriations committee. It is clear that the inmates are now running the asylum and have appointed the three stooges to be in charge.

Adult Adolescents

Is there any better proof that San Francisco and the Bay Area lead the civilized world in "adult adolescents" than the Bay to Breakers race or the How Weird Street Faire? Not all of our adult adolescents, however, are homegrown. They seem to gravitate here from all over the country (if not the world) due to San Francisco's reputation for being the place to be if the thought of growing up and acting like an adult is now what you're all about. There appears to be an epidemic of the Peter Pan Syndrome (I don't want to grow up) plaguing the entire San Francisco region.

Around here too many people go through adolescence, decide they like it, and opt to spend the rest of their lives in a similar state. What at one time was one of the premier distance races in America has degenerated into nothing more than an excuse for immature adults to behave as if they were still in high school. Exactly who came up with the idea of wearing idiotic costumes to a footrace? Some rocket scientist no doubt. In fact why not wear nothing at all? A chance to show off that incredibly attractive body perhaps? Our latest edition saw people dressed as a robot, a unicorn, a gorilla and several super heroes. Apparently few people came as normal human beings. That wouldn't be cool, hip or "off the wall."

San Francisco is so saturated with "colorful characters," "free spirits" and people with green, purple and blue hair (that's on one head, by the way) that these "unique individuals" have become commonplace. Twelve body piercings anyone? (Doesn't that set you off at the metal detector at the airport?) When you see these people around every corner it begins to get old, tired, trite and boring. They appear to have a strong desire to be seen and for other people to look at them and they endeavor to accomplish this with their shocking appearance and outrageous behavior. Perhaps they lacked attention when they were growing up. So they come to San Francisco and put on their act because it plays better here than in their hometown.

Those of us of a certain age can remember when the phrases "you'll like them, they're normal" and "down to Earth" were considered compliments. Not anymore. Don't dare call someone in San Francisco "normal" or "down to Earth" unless you want to be the recipient of a relentless verbal assault. Very few people in this city have any desire to be normal or down to Earth. Most simply want to be as strange as possible. Quite a few are having a considerable amount of success. They are also boring as hell.

Regarding "Moratorium on Executions Could End if Newsom Loses"

Should Gavin Newsom lose the recall election his successor would have every right to reverse the moratorium on the death penalty. California has 699 inmates on death row including 31 who have lost all appeals of their convictions and sentences.

Californians have voted to retain the death penalty four times in the last 49 years including 2012 and by a larger margin in 2016.

Proposition 66, which voters approved in 2016 sought to speed up executions by limiting appeals. In an amazing display of arrogance and hubris, Newsom signed an executive order suspending all executions.

Why put a death penalty proposition on the ballot when the governor can deny the will of the people and replace it with his own person agenda? Whatever happened to "The voters have spoken"? When the voters of California spoke Gavin Newsom didn't listen.

Ban Same-Sex Couples From Adopting? Of Course! Who Wants to Be Raised by My Two Dads? Or Moms?

IF YOU LISTEN TO NEW-AGE BULLSHIT FROM same-sex advocates and progressives of all stripes you may be duped into believing that two parents of the same sex can be just as beneficial to a child's upbringing as two parents of differing sexes. This simply isn't so. While parents of the same sex can be just as loving, caring and emotionally supportive as "traditional" parents the question here involves the "needs" of children and who can best provide what kids need to thrive. Kids need a male and a female role model in their lives to receive optimum emotional support. A child raised by "my two moms" will yearn, ache and pine for a father figure in their life and often feel cheated for lack of same.

As a boy I can't even imagine being raised by "my two dads." I'm sure it would be just as difficult for a girl when I think of what my mother meant to me growing up. Life without her would have been less than ideal (to put it mildly). When a child is ill who wants to receive tender loving care from Dr. Dad? No one!

Child psychologists and early childhood development experts will tell you children of a gay or lesbian parent may be more likely to have social and emotional problems. Much fewer children who are raised by same-sex couples live with their parents to the age of 18 and beyond. A better environment for a child growing up includes a parent of both sexes. Too many people are afraid to state the obvious, but not everyone.

Clueless Millennials

Somehow millennials have gotten the reputation for being clueless, unaware and only concerned with what affects them directly. A twenty something in the Chronicle's newsroom could not blame many of her friends for not voting because they didn't even know there was an election on Tuesday. Is it really fair to criticize millennials for not voting if they aren't aware that an election is taking place? Of course not! That would be like criticizing a parent for missing a child's high school graduation if they had no idea their child was graduating from high school, or not attending a parent's funeral if you were unaware your parent had passed away. Who knew?

I have to wonder how these millennials missed the news that there was an election taking place. It was in all the papers. Oh, I forgot. Millennials don't read newspapers, do they. Many don't even know what a newspaper is. They get all their news from the internet or on Facebook while sitting at their computers. Millennials only trust "reliable sources."

To be fair we should not criticize millennials for being apathetic but for being ignorant.

Becoming Inured to Tragedy

After hearing about the latest mass shooting at a Santa Fe, Texas high school we checked the Chronicle the next day for more details. Front page news? Apparently no longer. It wasn't until page seven that we found the story. This type of tragedy is now as commonplace as a suicide bombing in the Middle East. We are becoming numb and desensitized to the senseless loss of life our country is constantly being subject to.

For some reason more and more people are being born and raised who have no sense of right or wrong, no respect for human life and feel no remorse whatsoever for their evil, heinous actions. The number of people with serious mental/ emotional problems is skyrocketing. This is why we must make it as difficult as possible for these deranged individuals to acquire a firearm.

As it stands now practically every crazed lunatic with a persecution complex can obtain a gun and ammunition. It's harder to get a driver's license than it is to get a gun. It's time to stop talking about stricter gun control laws and do something about it. Then, perhaps, we won't be constantly reading about mass shootings in the newspaper.

Millennials Not Feeling Parenthood

WHAT A SHOCK! CALIFORNIA'S BIRTH RATE HAS dropped again to its lowest level in a century. As young adults continue to postpone having children or opting not to have kids at all. Fewer than 12 children were born per 1,000 California residents in 2017. That is about half of what it was in 1990. This makes perfect sense. Have you ever tried procreating while staring at a cellphone screen with your thumbs moving at hyperspeed with buds in your ears? Trust me, it's not as easy as it sounds, and if you ask me it doesn't even sound that easy.

As millennials have reached childbearing age they are not feeling parenthood. With a selfish self-centered "I'm the only person in the world that matters" attitude it makes no sense for millennials to have children.

Raising children properly requires an attention span that most millennials (quite frankly) lack. The latest studies clearly show your typical gnat possesses a greater attention span than your typical millennial. Since many millennials don't even drive a car and have no intention of acquiring a driver's license, how can they be expected to raise a child? Ever try raising a family without the use of a car? Good luck with that!

While the birth rate is down sharply for women under 40 it has actually risen slightly for women over 40. More good news! An increase in women giving birth whose reproductive systems have been breaking down for at least 15 years (the high end for optimum child bearing for a woman is 25 years old). Could this explain the sharp increase in children being born with A.D.H.D., autism and numerous other maladies that are on the rise? There has also been a sharp rise in children who require psychiatric counseling and have emotional problems. A birth rate that is half what it was only 28 years ago? How pathetic is that?

Also, becoming a parent would seriously eat into a millennials video game playing time. That would be simply unacceptable. Can you imagine a small child interrupting a millennial who was trying to record a personal best in their latest video game acquisition? Perish the thought! Millennials have their priorities in order and are not about to change. I recently asked a millennial if he was planning to start a family soon. His reply to me was "Is there an app for that?" I didn't have the heart to tell him there was not.

Ban Stupid Adults Instead

THE LETTER WRITER COMPLAINS ABOUT "constant noise from young children" ruining her flight. Most parents sympathize with other parents who have the chore of trying to keep their young ones quiet during a long flight having been there themselves. However, why single out children?

More often than being annoyed by kids we have been bedeviled by loud, boisterous adults who appear to enjoy hearing themselves talk. Often by the end of such a flight one sitting within earshot (which is practically the entire plane) will know the life story of the hot air filled blowhard.

Often they can be spotted standing up whenever possible facing in the opposite direction of their seat so they can face the people they are yapping at. I believe "holding court" is the perfect phrase to describe what they are doing. Inevitably they are boring as hell and would do us all a favor by sitting down and shutting the hell up.

As it turns out these are usually the same people who bring a suitcase on board too big to be a carry-on and spend an eternity trying to cram it into the overhead bin. I'll take a noisy kid over these adult buffoons any day.

I also enjoy watching the people who, as soon as the plane lands and they are able to, unbuckle their seat belts and stand up in front of their seat or in the aisle. The only problem is they aren't going anywhere for at least half an hour. Yet there they are standing (often hunched over) eagerly awaiting the opportunity to get off the plane as soon as possible. Being ridiculously uncomfortable for half an hour is well worth it if several nanoseconds can be saved getting off the plane. How about when you get on the plane and one's assigned group number is called the half-wits who jump up and run over to the line that isn't going to move for twenty minutes. I suspect they are so eager to get to their seat so they can cram their oversized carry-on in the overhead bin. Rather than a true carry-on what they have is a full-sized piece of luggage that, if it were measured, would be way too large to qualify as a carry-on. By doing so, of course they are denying others the opportunity to put their actual carry-on in the overhead bin because it is packed with oversized luggage. People behaving like selfish pigs? That would be an insult to pigs everywhere.

BART Station Facelift Behind
by 18 Months

Though the Powell Street BART Station facelift was scheduled to take five years it is already 18 months behind schedule. BART Director Bevan Dufty is quoted as saying "Things often move slowly and there are usually reasons." Really? Who knew? So there are reasons things move slowly. Unfortunately Director Dufty fails to divulge what those reasons might be. I can think of a few possibilities. Inept incompetence from top to bottom. I wonder if they are being paid by the hour. How about no sense of urgency (there never is). If the job was to complete a similar task in Los Angeles it would probably be a year and a half ahead of schedule rather than behind. That is because in Los Angeles the people in charge of getting things like the renovation of a BART station do not have their heads up their collective asses like they do in San Francisco. Judging from Mr. Dufty's casual matter-of-fact comment it is clear that Director Dufty regards incompetence, myriad SNAFUs, year and a half delays and "everything going wrong that can go wrong" as "the new norm," and to be expected. I propose we change San Francisco's unofficial sobriquet from "The city that knows how" to "The city that has no clue."

Courtesy and Manners

THIS IS NOT ANOTHER TIRADE ABOUT THE dirty mess the streets of San Francisco have become. Having just returned to San Francisco from a trip to Georgia and Alabama we were amazed by the polite, respectful, courteous and cheerful way we were treated by so many of the people we met. Those in the service industry as well as people we encountered by chance behaved as though we were long lost cousins they were thrilled to have found.

We heard the words "sir" and "ma'am" more often during our ten day stay in Georgia and Alabama than in our entire lives in San Francisco. Spending time immersed in this atmosphere was like a soothing balm for our souls.

Soon we were back in San Francisco. It was jarring (and not in a good way). Once again we were subject to the same rude boorish self centered behavior that is so typical of our area. Somehow the qualities that were so abundant in the south have been lost in San Francisco. It's funny how San Franciscans think of themselves as so hip, smart, sophisticated, savvy and politically correct. Too bad they haven't learned to treat their fellow human beings with courtesy and respect. Oh, by the way, the streets of San Francisco are still a dirty mess.

Pregnant Women Using Pot?
How Smart is That?

Some of us elderly curmudgeons are of the opinion that the latest generation of young people are more selfish and egocentric than Americans of the past. When I observe so many young people today and compare their values to that of "The Greatest Generation" who fought and won World War II. I can't help but wonder "What the hell happened?"

The article "More Pregnant Women Are Using Pot" is merely the latest example of young Americans acting like immature brats. Pot use by pregnant women has been linked to lower birth weights in newborns. Other studies have demonstrated the negative effect chronic use of pot has on young developing minds. Is it too much to ask of pregnant women to refrain from marijuana use during pregnancy for the sake of the health and wellbeing of their unborn child? Apparently so. What utter selfishness and total lack of self discipline and a moral compass.

Wake up and smell the kumquats. Think of someone other than yourself for a change. You might actually find it satisfying and rewarding. Who knows?

In Praise of Columbus

ONCE AGAIN SAN FRANCISCO'S ULTRA
progressive uber politically correct sensibilities are on full display. Our S.F. Board
of Supervisors decision to no longer honor Christopher Columbus by changing Columbus Day to Indigenous Peoples' Day is short sighted and myopic
at best. Columbus is considered by many historians to be one of the greatest
seamen and navigators of all time. His voyages to the West Indies led to lasting contact between Europe and the Western Hemisphere. Columbus made 4
historic voyages to the new world between 1492 and 1504.

Given the nickname "The admiral of the ocean seas" the courage, bravery
and determination he displayed in the face of incredible odds and constant peril
is truly remarkable. His voyages to America rank among history's most significant
achievements. His name has survived through the ages due to the importance
of his amazing explorations. Supervisor Malia Cohen, a sponsor of the bill to
rename Columbus Day "Indigenous Peoples' Day" said that dropping the official
Columbus Day designation was "incredibly important." Wow! That is amazing!
Do the S.F. Board of Supervisors realize that the seventh month of the Gregorian
Calendar is named for Julius Caesar? Time for another name change?

Atrocities Enough to Go Around

It's interesting that looking at history through our modern sensibilities European explorers such as Columbus, Cortez and Pizzaro have been demonized and are now considered anathema. It seems that when they arrived upon the shores of the Americas they disrupted an idyllic environment where everyone lived in peace and harmony. In reality this was not the case.

When Hernando Cortez arrived in Mexico with 500 Spanish soldiers in 1519 the Aztec Empire ruled by Montezuma was the dominant power in the region. The Aztecs were renowned for waging war on their neighboring tribes in Central and Southern Mexico. Montezuma I was a ruthless conqueror who would engage his enemies in warfare mainly for the purpose of capturing his adversaries alive so they could be used for human sacrifice or (if you will) ritualistic murder. Apparently their Sun God required human blood for nourishment. Priests would slash open the chest of a living victim and tear out the heart. After all, what's the point in slashing open the chest and tearing out the heart of someone if they are already dead? Worshipers often ate portions of a victim's body (lightly salted). Most victims were prisoners of war or slaves but the Aztecs also sacrificed innocent children as well.

When the Spaniards encountered the Aztecs in 1519 they did exactly what the Aztecs had done to their fellow Native American tribes. They declared war on them, conquered them and made slaves out of or killed their prisoners. The

Europeans and the Native Americans actually had a lot in common. There was more than enough inhumanity going on on both sides of the Atlantic.

Like it or not human history has been a history of stronger peoples conquering and subjugating weaker ones for land, wealth or religious ideologies. "Survival of the fittest" has been in vogue since the dawn of mankind. When the Europeans arrived in the Americas they brought guns, swords, horses, and germs that were unknown to Native Americans. They also brought an obsessive lust for gold and silver to bring back to Europe. To demonize people like Columbus over his amazing voyages of discovery is to look at history that has been distorted by the passage of 500 years. What Columbus did is viewed much differently today by non-historians today than it was in 1492.

There are two things that are certain in life: 1) Time passes. 2) Things change.

Dumb Phones

New Studies have shown a precipitous drop in happiness, self esteem and life satisfaction of American teens as their ownership of smartphones has risen from 0 to 73 percent. They are also devoting an increasing share of their time online. This appears to explain why a decades-long rise in happiness and satisfaction among U.S. teens suddenly shifted course in 2012 and declined sharply over the next 4 years. Some studies showed the greater the time spent engaged in online content and social media the unhappier the child.

Maybe it's time we finally acknowledged the harmful effects smartphones and internet addiction are having on our young people. Interpersonal relationships are suffering and there is an alarming lack of face to face communication. People rarely talk on the phone anymore preferring to text or email each other. I see people on dates spending most of the time looking at their cellphones while ignoring the person they are out with. How many people do you see with buds in their ears staring at their cellphones totally oblivious to the world around them? I have one question regarding the studies that show a decline in teen psychological well being, happiness and self esteem accompanying the rise of smartphone ownership and increase in time spent online. What about adults?

The Bottom Line

I THOUGHT FORMER MAYOR WILLIE BROWN made an excellent point in his "Willie's World" column on Sunday. "Most people think the National Rifle Association is a citizens group intent on protecting the constitutional right to bear arms. It is not. It's the political arm of a gun manufacturing industry intent on increasing sales," former mayor Brown said.

Once again in the great American tradition it's all about money. The N.R.A. is even opposed to raising the minimum age for purchasing a firearm from 18 to 21. I suppose their thinking is if someone is old enough to vote they are old enough to kill somebody. Just like the tobacco industry they want to get young people hooked on their product as early as possible. The death and destruction their product causes does not concern them in the slightest. Only the bottom line matters.

Towing Fees

I FIND IT INTERESTING THAT THE OUTRAGEOUS fees, fines and the cost of the ticket that have to be paid when one's car is towed when multiple tickets have gone unpaid is deemed unfair if it happens to a homeless person. Apparently it is considered acceptable if it happens to us "sheltered" citizens who can afford to be systematically robbed by the city and county of San Francisco.

If one is homeless a lawyer is retained and the city is sued because of the harsh treatment he or she has received. The rest of us can continue to pay the exorbitant fees that are charged if one receives a ticket as well as over-the-top charges for towing and impounding of the car. I'm trying to figure out why these fees are so much more than comparable cities like Los Angeles or New York. I can't help but suspect it has something to do with the obscene amount of money San Francisco throws into the bottomless pit called the homeless problem. Add to that programs to alleviate drug and alcohol abuse. No wonder there is no money left to pay our teachers a decent salary. If only teachers were as high a priority as the homeless or drug and alcohol abusers. Maybe then they could actually afford to live in the city where they teach, mentor and serve as role model to our children.

Stiffer Sentences Won't Hurt

READER R. VAN DYKE CAUTIONS AGAINST stiffer sentences for the perpetrators of smash and grab car burglaries. The thought being longer jail time might make these thieves "unemployable." Having been a victim of such a crime and knowing locals and tourists alike I'm afraid I have no sympathy for them whatsoever. They have absolutely no respect for private property and care nothing about anyone but themselves. The reader offers no solution to this "complex problem." The problem is, however, not that complex. What you have is a segment of the population who choose to acquire enough money to live on by smashing car windows, gaining entrance to said automobile and stealing everything they can get their hands on. Apparently having a real job and actually earning money the traditional way simply does not appeal to them. Preying upon innocent victims and creating hardship for them bothers these people nil.

Jail sentences making them unemployable? Seriously? These people already have a job. It is called "Career Criminal." That's what they do. No doubt a continuation of the "status quo" where these mindless criminals are slapped on the wrist and sent back out on the street to continue to ply their chosen trade is a better option than longer jail sentences. One thing I know for certain. They will find it considerably more difficult to smash car windows and steal what is inside from a jail cell than from out on the street.

Racial Disparity in
School Discipline

We have learned that 12.8 percent of African American males were suspended during the 2016-17 school year compared to 3.6 percent of students overall. "They are unfairly singled out" State Educator Professor Ed Wood said, "opening the door to the criminal justice system."

In truth there has been a mandate in the SFUSD not to suspend African Americans students if at all possible or the numbers would be even higher. While Blacks face discrimination and racism on a daily basis in our society those are not the main factors in the high numbers of suspensions, the achievement gap or the over- representation of African Americans in the criminal justice system. It is time to stop making excuses for poor African American performance in our school system. It is their disruptive unacceptable behavior that is causing the vast majority of these suspensions.

The root problem so many Black students face is a less than ideal home life and upbringing. Negative behavior begins at home just as good behavior does. Too many African American parents are failing their children by setting a bad example for them to follow. Too many Blacks are being raised by only one parent (often the mother). Ideally children need a father figure in their life and too many African American children never get that. How many Blacks do you come across that are being raised by their "Grandma"? Black kids need more parent involvement in their education. Black kids in the school lunch program show up to school in $200 tennis shoes that light up and glow in the dark like Stephan Curry's. Why not skip a day of school to go to the barber shop to have your hair arranged in cornrows?

Don't blame the SFUSD teachers for African American suspensions and the achievement gap when a chaotic unhealthy and often toxic home life is really to blame.

Looters Are Gonna Loot

Is THERE A MORE DESPICABLE FORM OF HUMAN life than looters? I am speaking of those who use the murder of George Floyd by a Minesota police officer as an excuse to loot, commit violence, burn anything in sight, smash windows, steal everything they can get their hands on and condemn all police officers as racist murderers to cloak their unlawful actions in the guise of protesting social injustice against African Americans.

These criminals know no shame. They are simply taking advantage of an atmosphere of utter chaos to commit their crimes hoping no one will notice.

To become a looter all self-respect must be abandoned (if any existed in the first place). All sense of right and wrong must be jettisoned if looting is to be done effectively. As in all human endeavors if looting is worth doing at all it is worth doing well. The chance to loot doesn't come along every day so that when it does one must take full advantage of the situation. It can take decades of diligent practice to master the art of smashing windows, burning autos and pilfering everything that isn't nailed down. Looting is best accomplished without a guilty conscience or (better still) no conscience at all. Not caring about anything but yourself, while not required, is highly recommended. As a looter, feelings of remorse or guilt will throw you off your game quicker than you can say "death to all policemen" and are to be avoided at all costs.

There is an old phrase that goes "How can you look at yourself in the mirror?" It is widely known that looters don't own mirrors. They prefer to smash them. Problem solved. Another saying that fits is "How do you sleep at night?" Looters don't sleep at night. They loot at night and sleep in the daytime. Another problem solved.

Growing up (like most children) I aspired to be a looter, but having a moral compass dashed my hopes and dreams. Imagine the beaming face of a proud child when on "Bring your father to school day" a looter shows up to explain to little Johnny's second grade class the finer points of his profession. The surprise on the faces of his classmates (not to mention his teacher) would be priceless.

So the next time a Black person is killed by a police officer for no reason (how long could that possibly take?) that is your cue to smash, burn, loot and commit wanton acts of senseless violence and mayhem, and even spit on the sidewalk.

What the Hell Happened?

Can anyone tell me whatever happened to all the tough, old school, hardass, no nonsense, say what they mean and mean what they say guys that used to be so prevalent back in the day? Though I wasn't on board with all of their sensibilities I have come to have a great appreciation for those people who are getting harder and harder to find these days. When I went to work at the Burlingame Post Office in 1976 the veterans who were nearing retirement were about my fathers age or even older. Having grown up in the 50's and 60's in San Francisco I was somewhat taken aback when I would witness a disagreement that couldn't be amicably resolved that would lead to someone suggesting to the other that perhaps they should "step outside" (no fighting on the workroom floor) to resolve their differences. While I believe every effort should be made to work out problems without such a confrontation a good old fashioned fist-fight is infinitely preferable to resorting to guns or knives and will result in very few fatalities and a limited amount of bloodshed. Many could be seen with a cigarette dangling out of the corner of their mouths, often not bothering to remove it while speaking. Perhaps so few can be found today because so many succumbed to lung cancer.

I suppose when one grows up during the depression and then has World War II thrust upon them it has a certain effect on one's character and world view. Many young people today have never had to endure any more hardship than having one of their electronic gadgets malfunction. (Into each life some rain must fall).

Nowhere can the difference between the attitudes of the men from my parent's generation and those of two generations later be seen than their behavior at their child "Back to school night" or "Open house." When my dad (and countless others like him) attended my and my brother's "Open house" at our grammar school, when the presentation was over he was sure to have a chat with our teacher. The gist of which was if my child does not mind you or gives you any trouble you have my permission to use (to borrow a phrase from the "Black Panthers") "Any means necessary" to keep my child in line (including the back of your hand). In other words the teacher was given "carte blanche" in regards to discipline. Children in the late 50's and early 60's tended to be better behaved in school than can often be seen today (I can't imagine why).

Fast forward two generations. If both parents attend their spoiled brats open house it is often the mother who has a chat with their child's teacher. The exchange nowadays tends to run along these lines. Mother to teacher: "If you should ever dare to so much as lay a hand on my "untouchable" offspring I will sue you for every penny you've got and do everything in my power to get you fired from your job and see to it that you never teach again." Many "New Age 21st Century" parents may take legal action if a teacher so much as raises their voice to their precious child. Children have begun to pick up on their parents' attitude by simply refusing to do what their teacher tells them because they simply don't have to. The school board has taken to pandering to these parents' whims for fear of another lawsuit. How did we go from "old school tough love" to incredibly easy to offend new age mothers in only two generations? What the hell happened?

I realize the entire country is not like San Francisco and these new age sensibilities do not permeate our nation from coast to coast. This is why so much of what goes down in San Francisco only serves to make us a laughingstock for the nation's amusement. Indeed, we have even discovered while visiting foreign lands when it is revealed that we hail from San Francisco, California people are amazed that we do not appear to be totally insane, can carry a coherent conversation and are quite capable of chewing gum and walking at the same time. Such is our global reputation (and deservedly so). To say it is embarrassing to admit where we come from would be a gross understatement. Often we try to change the subject or (better still) avoid it altogether. Why supply them with ammunition to ridicule, deride and mock us? Around here it is only a matter of time until a new edict is passed that defies belief (such as banning the use of the words, he, she, him and her, not only because it is offensive to people who do not identify with either gender but the terms are gender specific. Can't have that! I can't speculate whether the pendulum will ever swing back and we will once again see a return to "old school, tough-love, disciplined sensibilities or it will even get worse with these "mother from hell" producing prima donna children who are treated like royalty from birth, spoiled rotten, have every whim catered to and are protected from hardship like a moth in a cocoon while their spineless husbands look the other way.

"Birds"

Songwriters Elton John and Bernie Taupin are responsible for more hits than the mafia. The airwaves of America (and indeed most of the civilized world) were imbued with their music for the entire decade of the 1970's and beyond. One hit after another ensued from the music written by John (real name Reginald Kenneth Dwight) and lyricist Taupin.

It is not (however) one of their huge hits that concerns us here. One of their lesser known CDs contains a song entitled "Birds." In it lyricist Taupin delves into philosophical existentialism (whatever the hell that is) and raises fundamental (yet profound) questions that strike at the heart of our very existence. His words are timeless and yet as fresh and immediate as the latest mass murder committed by some deranged lunatic who had no problem getting his hands on an assault rifle and ammunition. Taupin writes:

"And everywhere I look

There's something to learn

A sliver of truth

From every bridge we burn

A hatful of quarters

And a naked song

Don't answer the question

Of where we belong

And everything I hear

Never makes any sense

Another old prophet

Perched on the fence

A cupful of pencils

And a self help guru

Don't answer the question

Of what I am to you

How come birds don't fall

From the sky when they die?

How come birds always look

For a quiet place to hide?

These words can't explain

What I feel inside

Like birds I need a quiet place to hide"

Taupin's words are enigmatic, quixotic, haunting, beautiful and yet disturbing all at the same time. After decades of rumination I would like to offer a possible answer to the question of why birds don't fall from the sky when they die. Let's say (for the sake of argument) you are a bird with one wing in the grave (soon to be followed by the other wing). I could easily imagine you might not be feeling up to flying at all and are in a nest in a tree, or (just as likely) being given "last rites" accompanied by friends and family. This scenario completely eliminates the possibility of a bird falling from the sky when it dies. It is (at the very least) a possible answer to this age-old question.

Get Your Heads Out of Your Asses and Repurpose the Great Highway Back to Vehicular Traffic

Heather Knight is a Chronicle columnist, the rest of us are not. It is her short- sighted, myoptic opinions we are subjected to on a daily basis. She takes great pleasure in lecturing us that San Francisco has lost it's "ideals,""progressive bent" or "moral compass." Knight uses her newspaper column to push her own personal agenda and apparently cares nothing about the traffic mess created around the blocks adjoining the Great Highway due to its closure to cars.

The reopening of the Great Highway to motor vehicles will be a cause for celebration for countless San Franciscans seeking relief from traffic congestion. 19th Avenue, which is a mess under the best of conditions, now has lanes constantly closed due to roadway construction and is bumper to bumper most of the day. As you approach 19th Avenue you see signs warning us to seek an alternate route while reminding us that the Great Highway is closed. Does this alternate route they are suggesting involve a helicopter by and chance? There is also enough room right along the Great Highway for walking your dog and riding a bicycle and always has been.

Coincidentally, at the northern edge of the Great Highway there just happens to be one of the largest public spaces in the United States (if not the world) that is absolutely ideal for families, dog walking and bicycle riding. Just punch Golden Gate Park into your GPS. You can't miss it.

Building a thoroughfare like the Great Highway and then closing it to vehicular traffic would be like building a bridge between San Francisco and Marin and then, because of the Covid-19 pandemic, using it for dog walkers, bicyclists and skateboarding. Families, while strolling on the bridge could take in the beautiful views of San Francisco bay, the sailboats and the sun as it disappears over the horizon. Who cares about commuters who are trying to get home after a hard day's work? That should satisfy Heather Knight's San Francisco "ideals" "progessive bent" and "moral compass."

The Great Highway Issue

WITH ALL OF THE DISCUSSION REGARDING THE Great Highway being closed to traffic, and walkers, bicyclists and skateboarders being allowed to use it on weekends and holidays, several issues are rarely considered.

Proponents of "The Great Walkway" like to point to the environmental benefits of the closure. In fact allowing walkers, skateboarders and bicyclists to roam unchecked is causing the destruction of sand dunes on the west side of the Great Highway. The landscaping on the median is also being damaged with gaps from people crossing mid-block and not just at the crosswalks, helping to destroy the Snowy Plover habitat. Air pollution and traffic congestion have increased due to more stop and go traffic rather than cars going a constant 30mph with no stopping (or even slowing down) from Sloat Blvd to Lincoln Way, increasing commute times and reducing the time commuters spend with their families.

Closing the highway can delay emergency response times and can impede first responders trying to use the fastest route possible. An open Great Highway could also be crucial in the event of an emergency. All these factors should be considered when deciding the fate of the Great Highway.

Lee's Legacy

HEATHER KNIGHT INFORMS US THAT FORMER mayor Ed Lee's legacy is his teacher housing plan. I am not sure that is a legacy I would want my name attached to.

Of the 775 school districts in California San Francisco ranks 478th in teacher salaries, ranking behind such places as Fresno, Benicia, Gilroy and Stockton. SFUSD teacher compensation is so pathetic we are now starting to see homeless teachers. To purchase a median priced house in San Francisco requires an annual income of around 300,000 dollars. San Francisco's average teacher salary is currently $67,540.

I suppose it is appropriate, considering how woefully underpaid they are, that our teachers should be herded into a "Teacher's ghetto" or (if you will) a "Housing project." Ed Lee had seven years to do something about teachers salaries and got nothing accomplished. Instead he chose to throw hundreds of millions of dollars a year down the bottomless pit called the homeless problem rather than investing in our teachers and education. San Francisco priorities on full display. On the plus side with all those hundreds of millions of dollars earmarked for the homeless some of that money will inadvertently avail many of San Francisco's teachers since many of them can no longer afford a place to live. I hope these homeless teachers appreciate what Ed Lee has done for them.

Keep the Tradition of Christmas Trees

So it has finally come to this. Reader D. Gupta suggests we are not to purchase a Christmas tree.

The tradition of the Christmas Tree began in medieval Germany. By 1600 many German families decorated their homes with evergreens for Christmas. By the mid 1800's the custom of trimming Christmas trees had spread throughout the world. Today some form of Christmas Tree is part of every Christmas celebration.

We have been driving down to Half Moon Bay for decades to cut down our tree from one of the many lots that grow the trees just for this purpose.

The smell of the freshly cut tree permeates the living room. The tree is placed in water to keep it from drying out. Then it is time to string the lights through the tree and adorn it with our ornaments. The warmth, pleasure and enjoyment it brings to our household is priceless. Lastly a star is placed atop the tree. This star represents the star which led the magi to the town of Bethlehem where Jesus was born. Besides, without a proper tree where would Santa put all our presents?

Racial Disparity

WHAT AN INTERESTING AND CREATIVE WAY S.F. District Attorney George Gascon found to reduce the percentage of African Americans in our criminal justice system. Rather than tackling the myriad, complex and daunting reasons that 6 percent of San Francisco's population could account for 43 percent of the people booked into jail from 2008 through 2014, the district attorney chose a much easier route by getting prop 47 passed, he simply reclassified several crimes, including drug possession, from a felony to a misdemeanor. Now that these crimes are no longer punishable with jail time 6 percent of the population is only accountable for 38 percent of the people being booked into S.F. jails. Wow! What an improvement! D.A. Gascon is merely playing a numbers game to try and create an illusion of an improvement in the racial disparity that still exists.

I have a suggestion for District Attorney Gascon for further improvement in a similar vein to reduce the African American population on death row. Why not reduce the crime of murder in a drive-by shooting with an assault weapon in a predominately Black neighborhood which is drug or gang related from a felony to a misdemeanor? Voila! Fewer African Americans on death row.

An Eye for an Eye?

How nice that Governor Newsom made a "case for mercy" in announcing a moratorium on Californians death penalty. I have to wonder how much mercy was demonstrated by the murderers on death row who carried out the death penalty on their innocent victims. The death penalty is only recommended for the most heinous of crimes and usually requires "special circumstances."

Thanks to Gavin Newsom suspending the use of the death penalty golden state killer Joseph De Angelo will live out the rest of his life in prison. Though California voters once again approved the death penalty and even voted to expedite the process Govenor Newsom chose to ignore the will of the people. De Angelo had pleaded guilty to 13 murders and admitted to more than 60 rapes. The death penalty was created for people like De Angelo whose guilt is beyond question and his crimes are so dispicable. No feelings of guilt or remorse have ever been displayed. Unlike his murder victims De Angelo will continue to live and breathe thanks to Gavin Newsom. Does Governor Newsom really feel that De Angelo's life is one that is worth saving? Perhaps he is not familiar with a sacred text that recommends "An eye for an eye and a tooth for a tooth"?

Regarding "Mondrian House's Eye Catching Days Over"

WE ARE IN THE MIDST OF A GLOBAL PANDEMIC the likes of which has not been seen for more than a century. Climate change and global warming threaten the future of our planet. There is a national election looming that could determine the fate of our country going forward. Forgive me if I don't appear too concerned because the Mondrian House on the Great Highway in San Francisco was painted blue. Why would anyone possibly care what color scheme someone chooses to paint their house? Maybe the new owners did not like the Mondorian color style (there are people who don't). The color scheme used on a house is like art. There is no good or bad art. There is only art that you like and art that you don't like. It is purely subjective according to personal taste. That is why some people can look at a large canvass that Jackson Polluck flicked black paint upon indiscriminately and see a work of genius. Other people can look at the same canvass and assume a bratty child having a tantrum must have found a can of black paint and a brush and decided to vent his (or her) wrath on the available canvass.

I have a suggestion for petty whiners who are mourning the loss of the "iconic" Mondrian House on the Great Highway. Paint your own house in the Mondrian House scheme and find something important to worry about.

Priest Father Joseph Illo

I HAVE TO DISAGREE WITH THE LETTER WRITER who took exception to London Breed's criticism of catholic priest Father Joseph Illo. Father Illo called the Covid-19 pandemic a "political ploy" and chastised his parishioners for putting fears over faith and skipping mass to "avoid the remote possibility of dying of Covid." Father Illo also challenged the severity of the coronavirus and urged Catholics to avoid media reports which he said were aimed at unseating President Trump. After a wedding was held outside St. Peter and Paul Church the newlywed couple and at least eight guests later tested positive for Covid-19.

Illo also said coronavirus infection numbers and hospitalizations are "largely unreal." In 2015 parishioners protested his ban on girls serving on the altar mass. Illo drew national attention in Modesto in 2008 when he said that voting for Barack Obama, who supported abortion rights would necessitate a trip to the confessional.

Kudos to Mayor Breed for calling out this catholic priest who shows signs of gross incompetence. Is there some reason this person hasn't been defrocked by now? Do catholic priests become tenured at some point (like teachers) and can't be fired from their jobs? If he is not Donald Trump's personal priest he certainly should be. They are definitely on the same page regarding the coronavirus epidemic. An ostrich with its head in the sand is an image that comes to mind. Denying the severity of the crisis is the last thing we need to hear from someone who has influence in the community. His comments are not only uneducated but dangerous.

All pious catholics know that worshiping God doesn't have to take place in a church among a large congregation. God can be worshiped at home alone or with a few family members.

Priorities in Order (As Usual)

Despite ridership dipping to 12% of what it was prior to the coronavirus pandemic and facing a projected loss of 975 million dollars over the next three years BART's transit agency's workers got a 2.75% raise July 1st. The top salary for station agents and train operators is now 93,085 dollars a year, plus benefits. BART Board President Lateefah Simon said that the raise was the right thing to do. Really? Seriously? "I support paying our employees a living wage," Simon added.

Meanwhile members of the San Francisco Unified School District are expected to do the near impossible task of educating, being a role model for and mentoring our children while being paid a fraction of what BART employees earn. How much formal education is required to become a station agent or operate a BART train? Do these BART employees need four years of college and a B.A. degree? Must they complete a fifth year of college and acquire a teaching credential? Do they have to pass the C.B.E.S.T. and C.S.E.T. tests? How about 60 units beyond their B.A. to supplement their paltry salaries? Do they need C.L.A.D. certification to demonstrate the proficiency required to teach English language learners? I didn't think so.

Finding a quality educator who can effectively teach our children is a lot harder than finding someone who can operate a BART train. Another example of the San Francisco Bay Area's skewed, upside-down priorities. Only in San Francisco? I certainly hope so.

Regarding Board Member Sues District Colleagues

Rather than being apologetic, contrite and accepting being stripped of her position as vice president of the school board and being removed from her committees over the racist anti-chinese tweets she made in 2016, school board member Alison Collins chose to take the offensive.

In an amazing display of arrogance and hubris Collins is suing the school district and five board members who supported a no-confidence vote against her. Apparently she feels that 72 million dollars plus three million each from the five board members who voted against her is just compensation. Collins' lawyer Charles Bonner said the school board has seven days to call a special session and rescind the vote and write a public apology for its actions.

Instead of being grateful she wasn't removed from the board outright, as 5,400 people who signed a petition were calling for, she responded with threats and intimidation. I urge the school board to do what it should have done in the first place. Remove Allison Collins from the school board.

As People Stay Home Earth Heals

THERE COULD NOT BE A BETTER EXAMPLE OF the harm that human beings are doing to our planet than the healing the Earth has undergone since the coronavirus has forced people to shelter-in-place.

With so many people staying home and driving less and the closing of pollution spewing factories, smog levels are down as much as 50% in many areas. Unfortunately the Trump administration has done everything it can to undermine the environmental policies of President Obama. Donald Trump's pro-business agenda has been a disaster for the ecology of our planet. We need to heed the lesson the coronavirus has taught us about the disastrous effects of human activity on the health of our Earth.

With amazing improvement in the natural environment due to the decrease in human activity I can't help but wonder what the effect on our planet would be if humans were removed from the equation entirely.

An "A" Without Effort

It would appear that I attended school at the wrong time. Had my timing been more advantageous I too could have known what it was like to receive an A on one of my report cards, as so many of my classmates did. Alas, it was not fated to be.

It has been suggested that all high school and middle school students receive an A on their report cards because of the shortened school year due to the coronavirus pandemic. The students who worked especially hard to achieve an actual A grade up to this point will no doubt be thrilled that even the worst performing students who were earning a failing grade until Covid-19 came to their rescue will now be awarded with the same grade they get.

It would be much fairer to simply give students the grade they were earning when the schools were forced to close.

I'm equally sure teachers will be thrilled at the prospect of giving an A grade to students who didn't show up for class, refused to do their homework and failed tests on a consistent basis. Your typical teacher would (I'm sure) relish the opportunity to give an A grade to such a student. An A for everyone makes a farce out of the grading system and makes no sense whatsoever.

A King's Ransom on the Homeless

A LETTER TO THE EDITOR IN WEDNESDAY'S Chronicle found it ironic that the front page of the Chronicle carried an article about spending 100 million dollars to fix the Millennium Tower next to an article about homelessness and what it says about how, as a society, we spend our money.

The truth is San Francisco's latest budget proposal earmarks 364 million dollars on the homeless problem. Spending 100 million dollars to get the Millenium Tower fixed might be a better investment than spending 364 million dollars on a homeless problem that not only doesn't get fixed but doesn't even improve. The homeless problem is a bottomless pit that hundreds of millions of dollars is poured down with no results to show for it. The homeless are a never-ending problem with no relief in sight. Couldn't that money be spent on something that might actually show results?

If you are going to be homeless, why would you want to be homeless in the city that has the highest cost of living of any in the country? These people are light-years away from being able to afford a one-bedroom studio apartment. Wouldn't you want to live where there is a possibility that someday you might be able to have a roof over your head?

Regarding "Voters Trust Feelings on Crime Not Statistics"

JOE GAROFOLI TELLS US THAT VOTERS, WHO will be deciding Gavin Newsom's fate in the recall election, are reluctant to believe that crime is down even though statistics tell us that it is.

Just like statistics regarding the unemployment rate or how many Americans are living in poverty, statistics regarding the crime rate can and are skewed, juggled and slanted to "prove" whatever one's personal agenda happens to be.

If you've been the victim of a "smash and grab" car break-in, had your home burglarized, or been accosted by a mentally ill drug addict (or know someone who has) you don't care about statistics claiming that crime is down. Murder rates are near all-time high levels and we have a district attorney's office that routinely fails to charge violent criminals with the crimes they have committed, only to release them back out on the street with disastrous results. Statistics lie and liars use statistics to "prove" whatever they want you to believe.

Young People Don't
Shelter-In-Place

According to the San Francisco Department of Public Health the vast majority of coronavirus infections in San Francisco have occurred among people in the 18 to 50 year old age bracket. It is not hard to understand why.

Younger people are not sheltering-in-place as diligently as older people. They are more likely to be in public without a mask or gloves. Young people tend to think they are bullet-proof and couldn't possibly come down with or succumb to the Covid-19 virus and that the epidemic is a problem for older people.

Solitude or spending the day with just one or two people is not what young people are all about. Some young people can shelter-in-place during weekdays but when the weekend comes around they become zombies. It-Is-Saturday. Must-Socialize-With- Friends-My-Own-Age. It-Is-Sunny-And-Warm. Must-Go-To-Park-Or-Beach-With- Friends. Must-Consume-Food-And-Drink-With-Them. It-Is-What-I-Do.

If we are to eradicate the virus, all people need to be on board with the recommendations of public health officials and young people need to stop acting like zombies on the weekend.

A Hard Story to Listen To

AFTER HAVING BEEN EXPOSED TO COUNTLESS memoirs of a similar nature, I feel the need to voice my opinion on these types of "My life was so interesting, fascinating and awesome I simply must tell everyone about it" accounts.

A person named Rachel Kushner titles her book "The Hard Crowd" and for some unfathomable reason supposes that someone other than her immediate family members could actually care about what she has to say. Her teen and young adult years in San Francisco in the 1980's is the subject of her book and from the review I read it couldn't possibly be more uninteresting. She tells us of people who "smoked, went to rock concerts, did drugs and tended bar in dives where an old man slept in a bed near the pool tables. Wow! Really? She must be the first person ever who, in their teen and early adulthood, ever experienced people who "smoked, went to rock concerts, did drugs or tended bar in a dive."

I grew up in San Francisco in the 1950's and 1960's. By the time I entered High School I was sick and tired of hearing accounts from acquaintances about how drunk they had been, how much weed they had smoked or how little sleep they had got. Their attempts to impress me with how cool their life was only served to have the opposite effect. These banal idiotic ramblings had become old, tired, trite and boring. I had not yet begun my sophomore year of High School and already felt if I had to listen to one more story like Rachel Kushner's my head would explode. But wait. There's more (unfortunately). She goes on to describe her friends as "ratty delinquents looking for beer, weed and opportunities for theft and trespass… We partied with strangers which is what I spent a lot of my youth doing." I knew numerous such people when I was growing up. We called them "The Village Idiots" and wondered if they would ever leave adolescence behind and grow up. Many never did. She also tells us of drinking at the beach at night and freezing due to not being properly attired. It takes a real rocket scientist to figure out it's likely to be cold at the beach at night in San Francisco. How unique and groundbreaking to think of drinking at the beach at night. I doubt if anyone ever consumed as much of an ounce of alcohol at the beach until Kushner and her friends invented it. I can't help but wonder if Rachel and her friends also invented drinking up at Sigmund Stern Grove on the same historic evening. Judging from what I read of this book review, the entire premise of this book is neither interesting, enlightening, amusing or touching. I cannot imagine it would appeal to anyone with half a brain. Accounts like Rachel Kushner's are a dime a dozen (and overpriced at that). If you'll excuse me I have to get back to the new autobiographies by Judy Collins and Graham Nash. It seems that musicians in the 60's took drugs. Wow! Really?

Gender Neutral Toy Section? What the Hell For?

Once again we are presented with the solution to a problem that never existed. A.B. 1084 by assembly member Evan Low requires large retail stores to have a "gender-neutral" area or display for selling children's toys and items. Do we really need a "gender-neutral" area for toys? In reality all toys are gender-neutral as boys and girls have been playing with each other's toys since the dawn of time. Any gender child can and does play with any toy they choose to. Is it really necessary to politicize the selling of children's toys for the sake of being politically correct?

Mr. Low tells us that not having a gender-neutral toy section "reinforces outdated and harmful gender stereotypes and stigmatizes what's acceptable for certain genders." Wow! That's amazing! Not having a gender-neutral toy area does all that? Who knew? What a classic example of "new age psychobabble bullshit" signifying nothing.

Mr. Low cares absolutely nothing about children's welfare. He is simply trying to further his own personal agenda and asinine progressive sensibilities by using his position in the assembly to enact laws that serve no purpose.

Rather than obsessing over being politically correct, gender neutral toy areas and other meaningless minutia Mr. Low should concern himself with the reasons behind the steady decrease in the happiness level of our children and teenagers since the mid 1990's. About this time we started to see the advent of the internet, the social network, Facebook, a computer in every home and a cellphone in every hand. Could it be that our children can sense when adults in general and their parents in particular are taking political correctness, "gender-neutral toy sections, themselves and life in general way too seriously. We are constantly making life more complicated, complex and difficult, to the detriment of our children's welfare. It does not help our kids when adults micro analyze every aspect of society. We need to focus on what's important in life and not on P.C. obsession, gender-neutral toy areas and senseless laws that enhance the quality of life of absolutely no one.

Gun Background Checks Are
Not Being Done

MANY PEOPLE WHO ARE SICK AND TIRED OF
the devastation and carnage brought about by the abuse of firearms are advocating for stricter gun control laws. This (to me) makes perfect sense.

What doesn't make sense is the fact that the FBI never completes hundreds of thousands of gun background checks each year because of a deadline that requires it to purge them from its computers despite a report that raised alarms about the practice in 2015.

A breakdown in the system contributed to a shooting in Charleston, South Carolina that left nine churchgoers dead. The FBI did not complete more than 1.1 million background checks from 2014 through July 2019. Why do we have laws requiring background checks for gun purchases when they aren't even being done? While we push for stricter gun control laws it might make sense to enforce the ones we already have.

BART Ambassador Program

WHILE AN "AMBASSADOR PROGRAM" FOR BART, where employees trained in conflict resolution roam the system sounds like a good idea, I'm not sure how effective it would be in the real world. Otis R. Taylor Jr. compares the idea to Muni's transit assistance program which trains people to resolve fights on buses. How has that been working out? Have the problems on Muni been significantly reduced? Not so's you'd notice.

In order to make an impact on the violence and overall danger of riding BART what needs to be done is to make it as difficult as possible to enter BART without paying the fare. The vast majority of the people who are causing serious problems on BART are entering the system illegally and not paying to ride the trains.

If we can drastically reduce fare evasion violence and crime would decrease significantly. As it stands an agile 5 year old with half a brain can easily gain access to BART without the bother of buying a ticket. BART needs to install new entrance stiles to thwart would-be criminals.

Ranked Choice Voting

Once again, thanks to ranked-choice voting, the second most popular candidate has won an election. Chesa Boudin, who according to political analyst David Latterman had zero chance of beating Suzy Loftus in a runoff election is now our city district attorney. An amazing result considering Boudin secured a little more than a third of the first place votes.

"It is the highest profile, clearest example of ranked choice voting not delivering the results the city intended to occur," Latterman said. Isn't it time to eliminate ranked choice voting so the most popular candidate can actually win the election? Now we have a district attorney who has vowed to limit, if not eliminate prosecution for the types of street crimes that San Franciscans are up in arms about. Another item on Boudin's agenda is to do away with gang enhancements. Wouldn't want to discourage people from being gang members! Perhaps Mr. Boudin wants to avoid offending people in gangs or (God forbid) hurting their feelings. Let's face it, the last thing we need is pissed off gang members.

No wonder the police officers association spent more than 600,000 dollars to defeat Boudin. Thanks to ranked choice voting they failed.

A Profane Speech

After the Chronicle's recent article on politicians and other elected officials lacing their speech with profanities we now have SF Supervisor Sandra Lee Fewer chanting F__k The P.O.A. over and over again at an election night party for District Attorney candidate Chesa Boudin. To emphasize her point Fewer raised her middle fingers while flanked by progressive leaders. Her lame rationalization that we have all heard these words before is trite and beside the point. There are any number of words that I have heard before that I would prefer to hear as infrequently as possible. To say that this kind of behavior is unbefitting of an elected public official would be a gross understatement. Perhaps Fewer's vocabulary is so limited these were the only words she could think of to express her infantile opinion.

It is no wonder that the San Francisco Board of Supervisors is known more for petty infighting, endlessly worrying about "progressive" or "moderate" majorities and it's functional incompetence, than it is for getting anything of consequence accomplished. How several of these supervisors ever got elected in the first place is beyond my comprehension.

"The civility in politics went out the window in San Francisco a long time ago," said political analyst David Latterman. If the downward spiral continues we will soon be subjected to profanity laced shouting matches rather than political debates and discussions. If one cannot refrain from shouting obscenities at the top of their lungs they should not be allowed to either speak in public or serve on the board of supervisors. Removing Ms. Fewer from the board would be a classic example of "Addition by subtraction."

Family Pride Month?
Not in San Francisco

AUTHOR JOSH GOHLKE ASKS THE QUESTION where have S.F.'s values gone? He points out that strollers in San Francisco are more likely to contain a dog than a child. San Francisco has had the smallest percentage of children than any city in the United States for years. Author Gohlke blames the high cost of living but other equally expensive cities like Honolulu and New York have a much higher percentage of children than San Francisco. The difference is that those other cities have not declared a "war on families" like San Francisco has. From trying to eliminate cars and parking spaces (ever try to raise a family without the benefit of an automobile?), to refusing to pay our teachers a livable salary, San Francisco puts up roadblocks to raising children at every turn. Have you ever heard of San Franciscans celebrating a "family pride month"? A family pride week? Day? Hour? Minute? Second? (Nano-second?) Apparently parents with children are not prideful enough to warrant a celebration (or a multi-colored flag). To answer Mr. Gohlke's question of where have San Francisco's values gone? These are San Francisco's values.

Progressive Collusion

A LETTER WRITER SUGGESTS THAT THERE were more votes for "progressive" candidates Jane Kim and Mark Leno than for "moderate" candidate London Breed. There are several flaws to this asinine notion. Candidates' votes are not combined because they are both progressive. People run for office as individuals and are voted for as individuals. Some people lean progressive on some issues, moderate on other issues and may even be conservative at times.

Independents like myself refuse to be pigeonholed into any one political agenda. The truth is that London Breed got by far the most first place votes and the election wouldn't have been nearly as close if not for ranked choice voting. Many voters were turned off by Leno and Kim's collusion in telling progressives to vote for one of them with their first place vote and the other with their second choice. Though 80% of the Leno/Kim backers did just that it was still not enough to steal the election from the more popular London Breed.

Progressives need to keep in mind that people run for office and not political ideologies. People are who we vote for and elect to serve as mayor and not personal agendas.

Regarding "Dog Whistle Politics" and "White Privilege"

Is it now considered a crime to be a native San Franciscan? The letter writer of "Dog Whistle Politics" seems to think so. The author tells us that being a "so called native of the city" somehow makes Suzy Loftus a bad choice for city district attorney.

Mentioning the fact that she was born and raised in San Francisco does not demonstrate a "deep disturbing lack of self awareness of your privilege as a white person in the United States?" Apparently "White privilege" is the new buzz-phrase used by "People of color." In reality it is a thinly veiled form of racism used to denigrate Caucasians. Many "people of color" feel they cannot possibly be racist simply because they are…"people of color." They are wrong. They can be every bit as racist as any southern white who is still fighting the Civil War.

Throughout the letter it's obvious the writer's concerned with one issue only. Immigrants and immigration appear to be the only thing that matters. I wonder if the author just happens to be an immigrant? We are told to vote for Chesa Boudin "who is the only candidate sensitive to the issue."

I am concerned with all the issues that affect San Franciscans native or otherwise. Every day when we pick up the newspaper we see yet another article about immigrants, immigration, sanctuary city policy, the latest crime commit-ted by an illegal immigrant who was deported x amount of times only to make their way back to San Francisco, and someone who died at the hands of an illegal immigrant who is in California because sanctuary cities policy prevented ICE from doing its job. It's too bad many of these victims did not exercise their "white privilege." Maybe they would still be alive today if they had.

"Cop Resigns After Shooting, is Charged with Murder"

A WHITE FORT WORTH POLICE OFFICER WHO shot and killed a Black woman through a back window of her home has been rightfully charged with murder. Atatiana Jefferson was playing video games with her nephew when she was killed. What about the idiot neighbor who called a non-emergency line to report a door ajar? Who calls the police because a door isn't closed? Was there a draft?

The decision to involve the Fort Worth Police Department started a chain of events that ultimately led to the death of Atatiana Jefferson. No doubt if the "nosey neighbor" had minded their own business Atatiana Jefferson would be alive today. Does this person call the police when a sock is missing after doing the laundry? How about if the newspaper isn't on the doorstep by 6 a.m.? We need to involve the police as little as possible (especially when African-Americans are involved) or risk tragic consequences.

Think Outside the Rocks

Kudos to the residents of Clinton Park who have tried to discourage homeless people and public drug users from befouling their neighborhood by placing 24 huge builders on the sidewalk.

Of course in San Francisco the homeless and the drug users get all the sympathy while the neighbors who are trying to clean up their sidewalks are vilified as monsters. Really? Who the hell wants homeless people and drug users setting up camp on the sidewalk outside their house? I applaud the residents of Clinton Park for their ingenuity and creativity in their desperate attempt to rid their neighborhood of these undesirables. Sometimes you have to think "outside the rocks."

Personally I would have recommended a water cannon, but that's just me. We constantly hear of people returning to San Francisco from foreign cities and marveling at the clean streets and lack of a homeless problem. That is because those cities have laws against sleeping in public places at night and they are enforced. What a concept! People often simply do what they are allowed to do. In San Francisco they are often allowed to do whatever they feel like with no repercussions. A once beautiful city is becoming an ugly one and when people try to do something about it they are crucified. Welcome to San Francisco values and culture.

Obscene Pensions

IN A CITY WITH A NEVER ENDING HOMELESS problem, people living in RVs and vans because they can't afford rent, and teachers who are paid such meager salaries they are forced to live in someone's basement, it's nice to know we can afford to pay pensions of 200,000 dollars and up to people who no longer work. How generous?

How is it possible that some of these people are being paid more money than they were while they were working? Does it make sense to pay retired police, firefighters, politicians and myriad city workers so much more than teachers who are in the classroom actually doing their jobs?

Perhaps it's because only a pathetic 13% of the residences in San Francisco has a child under age 18 living there, that our children are such a low priority in the city. Who cares what you pay teachers when it affects so few of our citizens? Another example of San Francisco values and priorities.

Regarding "Measles Makes Grim Comeback"

695 CASES OF MEASLES HAVE BEEN RECORDED in the U.S. this year with outbreaks detected in 22 states. Helping to exacerbate the problem are ignorant parents who refuse to have their children vaccinated and shyster doctors selling medical exemptions to parents so their children can avoid inoculation. It is widely known that the IQ of your typical anti-vaxxer is between 25 and 75 points lower than the IQ of your typical human being.

Many struggle to chew gum and walk at the same time. You can usually spot an anti-vaxxer without actually having to speak to him or her. Dead giveaways would include foaming at the mouth, excessive drooling, unintelligible speech and a proclivity for eating dirt. Even the smartest amongst them also have trouble spelling with any precision. Words, such as a, it, up, the, car, be, dog, and cat can confound them no end.

Meanwhile, polio is making a resurgence in Pakistan, where an anti-polio campaign was suspended after violent attacks on vaccination teams resulted in the death of a health worker and two police officers. Militant threats and deep rooted superstition have resulted in many parents refusing to vaccinate their children. Scourges such as the measles and polio, one thought eradicated by modern medicine, are making a comeback due to parental ignorance. These vaccinations should be mandatory with no exceptions.

Cutting Prison
Population in Half?

Has Bernie Sanders lost his mind? He is now advocating cutting the prison population in half and ending mandatory minimum sentencing. I completely agree there are some people in prison who do not deserve to be there and if it was in my power they would all be freed immediately. On the other hand there are way too many people who should be behind bars but aren't.

With all the mass murders that seem to occur daily, police officers being killed and myriad people with no sense of right and wrong who have no problem acquiring firearms Bernie's plan is to put half of our prison population back on the street? People aren't likely enough already to be the victim of a crime at the hands of some incorrigible who cares nothing about the safety and welfare of others?

I have to laugh every time some progressive argues against prison sentences because having a record will make it harder for an ex-con to find a job. Find a job?! They already have a job! It's called "career criminal."" The vast majority of these prisoners, once released, will go right back to the life of crime that got them there in the first place. We need to increase the prison population rather than reduce it. There are way too many deranged lunatics with access to firearms on the streets as it is. It is a sad commentary on the state of parenting in America when we have so many people who are being born and raised who need to be removed from society. When one's brain is malfunctioning to such a degree it makes rehabilitation virtually impossible. Those whose lives can be turned around need to be identified and worked with by behaviorists in an effort to turn them into productive members of society. Reducing the prison population by half sounds altruistic but it would end up a complete disaster.

Regarding "Many Police Bypass States' Sanctuary Law"

Kudos to the police agencies who find ways to cooperate with ICE in the face of California's sanctuary state laws. In the wake of the latest instance of an undocumented immigrant (El Salvadoran Carlos Arevalo-Carranza) committing a murder that could have been avoided if not for California's sanctuary policy, it is clear that police agencies are tying to make our cities safer by circumventing sanctuary laws. If sanctuary laws can ignore immigration officials' desires to deport people who are in this country illegally, some of whom are committing crimes, why shouldn't police agencies ignore California's failed and flawed sanctuary state laws?

Just one death at the hands of an illegal immigrant is one too many. Time and again people who shouldn't be in this country in the first place are committing crimes and causing the death of our citizens. What part of "illegal" is so hard to understand? You either have the law or you don't. You can argue the immigration laws need to be changed but until they are the laws on the books need to be enforced. "The existing policy that allows predatory criminals to evade lawful deportation requests makes everyone less safe," county officials wrote.

Regarding "Slaying Exposes Rifts Over Policy"

IN THE ARTICLE ABOUT SANTA CLARA COUNTY debating sanctuary policy rules in the wake of an illegal immigrant being accused of the murder of Bambi Larson, Cecilia Chavez of "Silicon Valley De-Bug" is quoted as saying "We completely understand the tragedy of losing a life but we cannot create a policy based on one incident." One incident? Has Cecilia Chavez been paying attention or has she lost the ability to count?

How many people have to lose their life because of an undocumented immigrant before sanctuary state apologists stop referring to each murder as "one incident" or an "isolated case"? Multiple deaths can hardly be called "one" or "isolated."

It is only a matter of time, unless sanctuary state policies are changed, before another citizen loses their life because an undocumented immigrant was sheltered from deportation.

The Flintstone House

I SEE WHERE THE SNOOTY, SNOBBISH PEOPLE OF Hillsborough are suing the owner of the "Flintstone House" over "gaudy" backyard decorations including a herd of large dinosaur sculptures. We always check out the dinosaur collection as we drive by on 280 to see if anything new has been added.

How anyone could have a problem with these whimsical pieces I have no idea. Since the statues rest on the owner's property and are not lewd, profane or evil in spirit, why would anyone care? It would seem that the button-down conservative sensibilities of the town of Hillsborough has been offended by the unconventional artwork.

God forbid anything out of the ordinary should be visible to motorists driving by on the 280 freeway. If you pass by the street the house is located on the statues in the backyard are not visible. Is this some kind of horrible blight that needs to be purged from the landscape? What we have here is the very definition of a "frivolous lawsuit." No doubt it will be summarily tossed out of court by any judge on those grounds. Perhaps the wealthy citizens of Hillsborough should concern themselves with how to spend their fortunes rather than how a neighbor chooses to decorate her backyard.

SFPD Assaults 1st Amendment

I COMPLETELY AGREE WITH THE CHRONICLE'S editorial on Tuesday "SFPD Assaults First Amendment."

Are we living in Russia, China or North Korea? I thought this was the United States where the first amendment guarantees freedom of the press. SFPD used a sledgehammer to break into Bryan Carmody's house in the Outer Richmond, detained him in handcuffs for hours and seized computers, notes and more from his office. A freelance journalist, Carmody had sold the story of the circumstances surrounding the death of Public Defender Jeff Adachi to local television stations. When Carmody refused to divulge the source of his information it drew the wrath of the SFPD.

I thought San Francisco wa ground zero for anti-Trump resistance. Now it appears the SFPD is on board with Trump's anti-press "Enemy of the people" rhetoric.

Supervisors Pay

How can you possibly justify giving San Francisco's board of supervisors a 12% raise in pay when members of the San Francisco Unified School District remain grossly underpaid? The 15,000 dollar raise will boost the supervisors pay to 140,000 dollars a year plus benefits. Civil service commission president F.X. Crowley was quoted as saying "We need to pay city servants a wage so they can live and raise a family here." Apparently this is not also true of our teachers whose job it is to educate our children, who are paid a fraction of what our supervisors are paid.

Teachers are much more essential than our bickering, dysfunctional board of supervisors whose main concern is if the board is made up of a majority of "progressives" or "moderates," so they can advance their personal agenda. (God have mercy on your soul if you are a conservative in this town). Most board members appear to care nothing about representing the people in their district. Furthering their political ambitions is what appears to motivate them.

What we get for the 140,000 dollar a year salary of each board member represents the worst return on an investment since the Giants gave Bary Zito 126 million dollars for a seven year contract.

Traffic Fatalities

Regarding the soaring traffic fatalities in San Francisco, Board Director Cheryl Brinkman is quoted as saying "At the root of all this is bad driving." While bad driving is a major cause of traffic fatalities there are other factors that play a part in the number of people being killed on San Francisco's streets.

If you've spent much time in San Francisco you couldn't help but notice reckless bicyclists ignoring red lights as if they didn't exist and blowing through stop signs without the bother of slowing down. Cars have to stop at red lights and stop signs. Bicycles need to do the same. It's as if they don't get the fact that if a crash occurs between a bicycle and a car, the bicycle (and it's rider) is going to lose. Perhaps they think that little helmet on their head provides better protection than the 2,000 pounds of steel (and an airbag) that a motorist is encased in. I would advise cyclists to use more caution or we may be reading about them in the "Life Tributes" section of the Chronicle.

Then you have your typical idiot pedestrians who cannot seem to discern the difference between the red "Don't Walk" sign and the white "Walk" sign. Is it that hard? It would seem that saving a few seconds getting across the street is more important than saving their own life. You've seen them (or perhaps you are one). Just as the red number reads one they step off the curb to cross the street oblivious to the fact that cars are about to be entering the intersection from the other direction. Apparently their priorities lean more towards getting across the street than not being hit by a car.

Then you have the morons who like to cross intersections with buds in their ears while staring at their cell phones. Often these fools aren't even aware if the sign says walk or not. This attitude displays an alarming lack of curiosity. Take the buds out of your ears and put your cell phone away and you might be able to hear and see what is going on around you.

There are many reasons for San Francisco's high traffic fatalities. To put the blame solely on drivers does not tell the whole story.

Let the Poor Drive Drunk

I LOVE THIS LIBERAL PROGRESSIVE POLICY. THE 2,000 dollar fine for receiving a DUI will now be waived if one does not have the means to pay it. After all, poor people should have the same right as our more well-to-do citizens, to consume 2 ½ times the legal limit for blood-alcohol content, then hop into their automobile and put themselves and other motorists and pedestrians in danger of being killed.

Isn't the 2,000 dollar fine meant to discourage and punish driving while intoxicated? Should someone who lacks the money to pay such a fine be spending the little money they do have on getting drunk on alcohol? Is it just me? Perhaps a person with limited financial means should be especially careful not to waste what they do have on liquor and then drive while drunk. Ya think?

The lesson that has been taught to Ramon Wence-Valladolid is a simple one. Go ahead and get drunk and drive while intoxicated and the 2,000 dollar fine will be waived because you are poor. If fines for drunk driving should be waived for poor people then shouldn't all fines be waived if you do not have the means to pay them? We should have a "no fine" threshold so that people under a given income level would be issued a license exempting them from paying any type of fine. If a police officer tried to cite a poor person for driving 100 miles per hour in a 15 mil an hour school zone (when children are present) they would have to think again. By simply whipping out their "no fine licence" they would be on their merry way. The poor also would no longer have a problem getting rid of their unwanted trash or garbage since they would no longer be susceptible to fines for littering. Simply dump all of your crap wherever the hell you feel like and let the street sweepers worry about it. Let's face it, the poor have enough problems as it is. How to dispose of their refuse should not be one of them. No more fines for not paying taxes, parking in a handicap parking space, or even paying for an overdue library book, would help to ease the pain of being penniless. There are literally hundreds of instances where a "no fine licence" would come in handy. So go ahead and drive drunk. Assuming you don't have the money to pay for the fine.

Sanctuary City Laws

How many more violent crimes and murders have to occur before California's liberal progressives admit California's sanctuary cities law is a well meaning but failed policy? Along with allowing immigrants who deserve a shot at a better life to stay in this country, we are also harboring people who are committing crimes that are shattering the lives of families such as that of Roul Singh.

An illegal immigrant who should not have been in this country is the latest perpetrator to take the life of an innocent victim. I am sick of the hollow excuses and rationalizations used to justify our sanctuary city's policy. San Francisco Immigration Attorney Bill Hing is quoted as saying "This situation is more about what the person's state of mind was and how he got into this situation and it has less to do with the fact he is not a citizen." What the hell does that even mean? Talk about mindless babble that means nothing! Obviously more smoke and mirrors designed to obscure the fact that an illegal immigrant who was shielded from deportation due to sanctuary cities law has committed yet another killing. These laws that prevent violent criminals from being deported have accomplished the near impossible. They have made Donald Trump look smart.

The Great Highway Problem

I BELIEVE I HAVE AN EQUITABLE SOLUTION TO the Great Highway problem. Now that the Great Highway has been reopened to vehicle traffic families, bicyclists, skateboarders and walkers (dog and otherwise) who are directionally challenged and cannot seem to find Golden Gate Park or Ocean Beach (they are both notoriously difficult to locate) need an outlet for their activities. I propose we simply close the Golden Gate Bridge from 5 a.m. Monday morning until noon on Friday to vehicular traffic. This would allow the aforementioned individuals to walk, skateboard, bike ride or picnic right on the Golden Gate Bridge free of traffic in either direction. Excellent views of the bay are afforded from either side of the span. If this compromise should create any traffic congestion, tie-ups or hassles for commuters they will simply have to adjust and learn to live with it by finding alternate routes. Voila. Problem solved.

Regarding "Strong Health Systems Could Limit Violence"

The letter writer tells us that "countries that have more guns per capita than the United States but no killing rampage have strong health systems." Is there someone on this planet that doesn't know that there aren't any countries that have more guns per capita than the U.S.? If so they must live in a cave like John the Baptist. The country with the second most guns per capita is the Falkland Islands with a little more than half the gun ownership of our country.

Improving mental health care is crucial but there always will be people with mental health issues. There always has been. There are now. There always will be. It would be much easier to eradicate firearms than to eradicate mental illness. The most vital action the government can take is to make it as difficult as possible for every deranged lunatic with a persecution complex to acquire a firearm and ammunition.

"These Tragedies Happen All the Time"

OF ALL THE STATEMENTS MADE IN THE AFTER-math of the controversial acquittal of Jose Ines Garcia Zarate, of Kate Steinle's murder, the most curious (to my mind) was made by Jonathon Simon, director of the UC Berkeley Center for the Study of Law and Society. "These tragedies happen all the time," he was quoted as saying. Really? All the time?

A homeless undocumented immigrant who had been deported back to Mexico five times and had drug convictions in the U.S. was released from a San Francisco jail before the shooting under the city's sanctuary city policy. He then finds a gun, goes to the crowded Embarcadero, causes the gun to discharge resulting in the death of Kate Steinle in front of her family and dies in her father's arms. Happens all the time? Seriously? In which alternate universe does Jonathan Simon live in? Certainly not the one the rest of us are occupying.

In the wake of all of the fallout surrounding the jury's decision I think inane, asinine comments like the one made by Mr. Simon should be kept to a minimum.

The requirement of an involuntary manslaughter conviction is a finding that Garcia Zarate caused Steinle's death with an unlawful, negligent act. Am I missing something here? Was there anything that Garcia Zarate did that day that was not unlawful or negligent? Yet he isn't convicted of involuntary manslaughter?

What was the jury thinking? Were they thinking? Federal authorities unsealed a warrant for Garcia Zarate's arrest and plan to deport him for a sixth time. How long could it possibly be before he is back on the streets of San Francisco?

"People of Color" Aren't We All?

Isn't it time we put to rest the idiotic phrase "People of Color"? It has appeared numerous times in the Chronicle recently and I'm still trying to grasp it's exact meaning. Unless I'm mistaken every person on Earth is a "person of color." Show me someone who is totally devoid of color and I'll show you someone from another planet (if not another one of the eleven universes predicted by string theory). The only possible exception would be Black people. As we learned in Jr. High School black is defined as the absence of color. The people the phrase pertains to most would be White people since white is a combination of all colors. I'm pretty sure this is not the intent of the people who use this phrase.

Isn't it time we dropped all these ridiculous labels that only serve to separate and divide us? Who cares whether a person is black, white, brown, yellow, red or any other shade or hue? Do you want to spend your life being a color or a human being? Instead of dwelling on our differences, why not emphasize our similarities? All labels do is set people against each other and create friction and discord. I am sure such a day is on the horizon but (on my doctor's recommendation) I have opted not to hold my breath.

Feinstein's Civility Not a Liability

I AM AMAZED AT SOME OF THE CRITICISM Senator Dianne Feinstein has received in recent weeks. Brian Fallon, director of Demand Justice, is quoted in the Chronicle chastising Feinstein for "clinging to a bygone era of civility and decorum that Republicans abandoned long ago." When did acting with civility and decorum become a liability rather than an asset?

Perhaps Fallon would prefer Democratic leaders to act like President Trump and throw a temper tantrum when things don't go their way. Disagreements between the parties could be settled by obscenity-laced tirades and shouting matches. Don't forget good old fashioned fisticuffs as a way to settle problems. Why not revive the old custom of simply fighting a duel (pistols at ten paces)?

It may be time for Senator Feinstein to retire from the political scene, but if it is, it is not because she treats everyone (including Republicans) with dignity and respect.

Justice Is Served?

In 1963 WILLIAM ZANTZINGER WAS RESPON-
sible for the death of Hattie Carroll. The murder occured at a hotel in Baltimore.
Zantzinger was a socially prominent tobacco farmer from southern Maryland.
He became drunk at a charity ball and struck Hattie Carroll with a cane. Later
she collapsed and died of a stroke. The ball took place at Baltimore's Emerson
Hotel. Zantzinger was arrested and charged with homicide but the charge was
later reduced to manslaughter. Zantzinger was born into a wealthy family who
could afford the best lawyers money could buy. The family was well known in
political circles in Maryland and was well connected with friends in high places.
Zantzinger showed no remorse for his actions. Hattie Carroll was a domestic
worker and the mother of ten children. She had no wealth, no political connections and no high society friends. William Zantzinger was out on bail in a matter
of minutes after his arrest so he could continue to live his privileged life with as
little interruption as possible.

When the trial commenced many witnesses who saw the killing occur testi-
fied against Zantzinger. This (apparently) made no impression on the judge who
handed down a sentence of 6 months and a fine of $625. This incident was chron-
icled in the song "The Lonesome Death of Hattie Carroll" by Bob Dylan © 1964.

Fast forward to San Francisco in the year 2017. "High profile" political
consultant Enrique Pearce is arrested and charged with possessing more than
600 child pornography images, some portraying sexual sadism and masoch-

ism. He pleaded guilty to a crime that often results in a sentence of decades in a state penitentiary.

Pearce once held lucrative contracts with Mayor Ed Lee and other San Francisco politicians. He was also charged with driving under the influence of alcohol to which he also pleaded guilty. Pearce's McAlister Street apartment was raided in May 2015 when authorities confiscated devices with photos and videos of boys as young as infants being held down and raped.

Judge Rene Navarro handed down a sentence of 6 months in the county jail for Pearce's heinous, malicious and cowardly crimes. I suppose it is appropriate that William Zantzinger and Enrique Pearce should receive identical sentences for their inhuman actions.

There is a perception of San Francisco as a super progressive, uber politically correct city with a fair and balanced criminal justice system. Nothing could be further from the truth. There is nothing progressive or politically correct about slapping the wrist of a man whose life appears to revolve around the exploitation of children as young as infants for his own perverted gratification with no concern for the young lives his behavior could be destroying and the lasting effects of the mental, physical and emotional trauma endured by these innocent victims.

San Francisco of 2017 has much in common with Baltimore, Maryland of the early 1960's. Those who have political connections, wealth, friends in high places and high-priced lawyers who are masters at plea bargaining and downplaying the seriousness of the crime that was committed (as well as lying with a straight face) and (mis)interpreting the law for their own gain are not treated the same as those who lack all these advantages. The wheels of justice do not turn the same for all people. William Zantzinger and Enrique Pearce, lacking all of their clout, would have spent decades behind bars instead of the ridiculously light sentences they received. Judge Rene Navaro would have fit in well in the criminal justice system of Baltimore, Maryland of the early 1960's. It is amazing how little things have changed in the ensuing five decades.

Regarding "Disturbing Case Tossed in the 'Interest of Justice'"

After a 15 year old girl was harassed, molested and terrorized for half an hour in the West Portal neighborhood by Bill Gene Hobbs, the girl's parents were understandably irate over charges being dropped by San Francisco Superior Court Judge Russell Roeca. A court order to stay away from the girl was also wiped out. Judge Roeca's ruling was "In the interest of justice." In what sense does this ruling convey justice?

This decision is consistent with Chesa Boudin's District Attorney's Office's lack of concern for the victims of domestic violence. The girl's father, Erin Zarega, asked to be kept up to date in the case and was "before everything got bogged down in delays and reschedules." Amazingly the District Attorney's Office chose to charge the child molestation as a misdemeanor rather than a felony.

Records show that Hobbs has had six criminal cases against him in San Francisco dating to 2017, including trespassing, and giving false information to police. They were all dismissed by judges "In the interest of justice."

Where do I sign the recall Chesa Boudin petition?

No More Chinese (Corruption)

WE RECENTLY HAD A REPORT OF A MOST distressing occurrence in San Francisco the other day. Someone had scrawled "No More Chinese" on a building in the downtown area. This kind of racist, biased, intolerance has no place in modern society. I had hoped this type of bigoted racism was a thing of the past but apparently it is not so.

If, however, the graffiti had been amended to read "No More Crooked, Corrupt, Dishonest Chinese Politicians" I can hardly see how anyone could object.

Too many elected and appointed politicians and officials in the city deal in bribery, graft, selling favors and extortion as a means of padding their already bloated salaries. It is not that the Chinese are the only ones who deal in these illegal activities. Far from it. Politicians of all races, colors and creeds have been known to partake of these endeavors. The Chinese have elevated these types of crimes to an art form, perfected the stratagems by which they can be accomplished and simply took it to another level.

They have transplanted myriad white-collar crimes from China and Hong Kong to San Francisco without missing a beat. Many have been arrested, tried and found guilty of corruption with (no doubt) more to come. We need to break the cycle of "pay to play" politics that is so deeply embedded and pervades San Francisco government.

An Eye for an Eye

Regarding the letter writer who speaks of "Intolerable Injustice."

The death penalty can be implemented without innocent people being executed. Only when guilt has been proven beyond the shadow of a doubt should this sentence be carried out.

If the letter writer believes that all children are "playful, fun loving and basically kind" he simply hasn't been paying attention or has spent very little time in the company of children. At times certain kids can be especially cruel, mean and vicious. The threat of punishment for unwanted behavior is crucial in effectively raising children. Most parents are well aware of this fact.

He speaks of a world of peace and happiness free of senseless killings. Sure sounds nice. Unfortunately such a world would also be free of human beings as well. Though "pie in the sky" platitudes such as these are awesome to listen to (and easy to say) they have nothing to do with the real world we are fated to live in. In the real world incorrigibles, criminals and perpetrators of evil need to be punished for the crimes they commit.

There are 330 million people living in the United States. If only 1 percent of the population has a serious mental/emotional disability or is capable of violent behavior, you would be looking at 3 million 300 thousand potential people who have no respect for the laws of the land or their fellow human beings. There are currently 2.2 million people incarcerated in the United States. When you subtract the young children and infants from the population total the fact is there are still many people on the loose who (in a perfect world) would be behind bars.

Those who callously, wantonly and for no good reason take someone's life, their own life should be forfeit. When the subject of the death penalty was voted on Californians voted for it and also passed an initiative to expedite the process by which murderers could be executed. Governor Gavin Newsom (in his infinite wisdom) chose to ignore the will of the people and suspend the death penalty. So much for majority rules. Is this a democracy or are we being ruled by King Gavin Newsom I? Apparently he sees himself as a kindly parent who has to make decisions for his uninformed children who are incapable of thinking for themselves. Why do we bother to go to the polls on election day to decide such matters when, with the stroke of a pen, Gavin Newsom can defy the will of the people. An amazing display of arrogance and hubris.

An Irrelevant Life?

IN WHAT MUST RANK AS THE MOST BRAIN-DEAD and historically inaccurate statements I have ever heard, the Board of Education tells us that Abraham Lincoln's life, taken as a whole, "Was not relevant." Not relevant? Abraham Lincoln?

Lincoln is credited with preserving the American Union during the Civil War. He led the country through the gravest crisis in our nation's history and proved to the world that democracy could be a lasting form of government. He signed the Emancipation Proclamation and made two of the most powerful and insightful speeches in our nation's history; the Gettysburg Address "government of the people, by the people, and for the people shall not perish from the Earth" and his second inaugural speech, "with malice toward none and charity for all… we must bind up the nation's wounds."

His brilliant words have echoed down through history. Given the climate of the times, had not Lincoln been president the 265 indigenous men whose death sentences were commuted may have suffered the same fate as the 32 that were executed. Perhaps the Board needs to reassess what constitutes a "relevant life."

Regarding "Elite S.F. School May Shift to Lottery"

I SEE THAT SAN FRANCISCO HAS MADE THE decision to "dumb down" the admission requirement to get into Lowell High School by instituting a random lottery system for admission. Thanks to the board of education soon Lowell will regress from one of the top performing public schools in the country to just another mediocre, run of the mill, under-achieving high school like most of the SFUSD.

No mention is made of Ruth Asawa School of the Arts where admission is based on competitive auditions and there is a distinct lack of diversity. Is admitting students based on their artistic ability any different than admitting students based on their academic ability? It would seem that the school board feels that it is preferable to have no outstanding academic high schools in San Francisco than to have only one.

Covid-19 Distribution

To paraphrase an old saying, the rich get healthy while the poor get sick. The inequities engendered by the wealth gap among the nations of the world can clearly be seen by where the coronavirus vaccine is most prevalent and where it is not.

The United States and other wealthy countries are scooping up the world's supply of the Covid-19 vaccine. Poorer nations without the means or know-how to obtain the vaccine are struggling to procure their share with little success.

The World Health Organization recently warned that this disparity has put the world "on the brink of a catastrophic moral failure."

It is unconscionable that the poorer nations of the world will be the ones suffering the most throughout the Covid-19 pandemic.

Colored People or People of Color

WHEN WE WERE GROWING UP IN THE 50'S AND 60's a common phrase that was used to describe the Black race was "colored people." As time went by the phrase began to take on a racist overtone and was eventually considered to be a biggoted, brain-dead and clueless way to refer to our African-American population. The phrase all but disappeared from common usage, except (of course) from isolated pockets of the rural south where it continues to flourish to this day.

Several decades passed and (hopefully) a more heightened sense of racial sensitivity has evolved leading to a much different way to describe those whose descendants are from the African continent. As one would hope this modern expression is totally devoid of racist shadings, condescension or intolerance of any kind.

The offensive, rude, abhorrent "colored people" has been all but replaced by the much more socially aware "People of color." See the difference? It is astounding how the word "of" can completely transform a phrase from a horribly offensive one to a phrase that is totally acceptable. Amazing.

So in the seven decades that have elapsed since the fifties we have made the quantum lead from "Colored People" to "People of Color." That's what I call progress.

Regarding "Progressive Prosecutor Quits, Joins D.A. Recall"

Often when a politician is facing a recall election his or her friends, backers and colleagues circle the wagons, issue statements backing their beleaguered associate and offer any kind of assistance they can. Members of District Attorney Chesa Boudin's staff have chosen a different approach.

Former homicide prosecutor Brooke Jenkins, one of about 50 attorneys to leave since January 2020, when Boudin took office, has opted to volunteer to aid the campaign to recall Mr. Boudin. Not exactly a ringing endorsement for her former boss.

With so many resigning from the district attorney's office it has left many units staffed by people with little experience. No one still working in the homicide unit has ever secured a murder conviction in San Francisco and nearly half have never tried a murder case. The sexual assault unit is similarly staffed mostly by people without even a year of experience prosecuting sexual assault cases.

In a telling response to these criticisms Mr. Boudin said the "most important" units are staffed by career prosecutors. Apparently the homicide and sexual assault units do no qualify to be considered among the "most important" units in Mr. Boudin's district attorney's office. This makes me wonder which units are the most important that Mr. Boudin refers to.

How to Achieve Immigration Reform? Block Traffic on the Golden Gate Bridge

SAVVY IMMIGRATION REFORM ACTIVISTS HAVE shrewdly surmised that the most effective way to achieve their goals is to (what else?) prevent traffic from flowing smoothly on the Golden Gate Bridge. It is widely known the likelihood of immigration reform is directly tied to the ebb and flow of traffic on San Francisco's landmark span. While this may seem counterintuitive to most people with half a brain it does not to your typical illegal immigrant. They are keenly aware that legislators in Washington D.C., who can actually do something about immigration laws, (and are three thousand miles removed from the Golden Gate Bridge) are thrown into a panic attack, experience heart palpitations, become overwhelmed with grief, and seriously consider suicide whenever traffic on the Golden Gate Bridge slows in the slightest increment. Just why legislators in D.C. should give a "rat's ass" about the traffic on a bridge on the other side of the country remains unclear, but there is no denying it is so. Another pertinent factor is that the ones most responsible for our country's immigration policy are the very same people who use the bridge to get from San Francisco to Marin and vice versa. Hence the need to punish these commuters appropriately. It is known far and wide that the surest way to get someone to be sympathetic to one's cause is to prevent them from crossing the Golden Gate

Bridge in a timely fashion. The longer the delay incurred, the more fervent the new adherent becomes. If cars have to be abandoned mid span because traffic has come to a total standstill is when motorists are at their most sympathetic. Who wouldn't want people who are hell-bent on disrupting the morning commute from achieving their goal of citizenship? Endearing themselves to our society in such a manner has been incredibly effective over the years. This can plainly be seen by the level of immigration reform that has occurred during the last several administrations. Perhaps if they got the hell off the Golden Gate Bridge and allowed people who have nothing to do with their plight to cross the bridge and get to their jobs, people would view them in a more favorable light.

Regarding "S.F.'s Outdoor Music - And Irate Neighbors"

I CAN DEFINITELY SYMPATHIZE WITH ANNOYED neighbors who are complaining about the loud music being played at food truck sites in the city. A persistent problem in large urban areas such as San Francisco is the constant presence of loud intrusive noise which adversely affects our quality of life. For business owners to ascribe complaints over excessively loud music to being targeted because of their race is heavy-handed at best.

I think that most people can agree on the fact that one man's (or women's) music is another person's noise pollution.

Life Imitates Art

Those of us who are familiar with the classic H.G. Wells' book "The Time Machine," which was made into an excellent movie, know the scene where George first encounters the people of the distant future called the Eloi. He sees them lounging in the sun by the banks of a river. Then he notices a young woman being swept along with the current in danger of drowning. No one lifts a finger to try and save her and George cannot understand why they are unconcerned. He dives into the water saving her life. Since no one lives past young adulthood the Eloi have devolved into unfeeling zombies who do not care about the fate of their friend.

Authorities in Florida say a group of teens watched and laughed as a man drowned in a retention pool. Jamel Dunn drowned in the city of Cocoa on July 9th. Police said a group of teens recorded the 31 year old's drowning. The teens can be heard laughing at Dunn and telling him he was going to die and they weren't going to help him.

For these five teens to have absolutely no compassion for a fellow human being is beyond pathetic. Who the hell are these people and who raised them? To say that their parents instilled no moral values in their children would be a gross understatement.

Apparently some people have devolved into the Eloi of the H.G. Wells story and have no regard for human life, and are amused by the drowning death of a fellow human being.

Far too many parents today are doing a horrible job of raising their children. There are those who think that the human race has ceased getting smarter and we are now seeing an alarming trend of young people with less intellect and common sense, a shorter attention span, are uncaring, concerned only about themselves and have no compassion for others.

A Modest Proposal on
Teacher Salaries

THERE HAS BEEN A LOT OF TALK ABOUT HOW
underpaid San Francisco's teachers are and how we are losing so many teachers
to other school districts because they cannot afford to buy a house or pay the rent
for an apartment on the meager salary they are paid. A serious teacher shortage
has resulted.

I have a suggestion that just might solve the problem. While it is arguable
whether or not apprehending criminals or putting out fires is worth tens of thousands of dollars a year more than teaching, mentoring and being role models for
our children, I'm sure most people would agree that performing the duties of a
public school teacher is worth at least as much as not arresting perpetrators, not
extinguishing fires or not performing the functions a hundred other jobs in the
city government. All we need to do is tie teachers salaries to the pensions that
these ex-city workers are being paid. Then our teachers could finally afford an
apartment (if not a house) of their own in the city where they teach. A simple
solution to a complex problem. You're welcome.

How Dumb Are We?

As if we need more proof that this current generation of Americans is more clueless, brain-dead and self-absorbed than any generation of humans since Neanderthal man was roaming Europe, Asia and Africa 100,000 years ago we now have it. (Neanderthal man is now considered a subspecies of Homo Sapiens, kind of like Dodger fans).

U.S. Coast Guard stations that watch over the Great Lakes have seen a spike in "fake distress calls." The Coast Guard said that more than 160 hoax calls have been made across the Great Lakes this year. That's nearly triple the number they had at this time last year. Captain Joseph McGilley of the Coast Guard's unit in Cleveland says hoax calls can put boaters at risk because they can divert search and rescue responders during real emergencies. Really? They can? Who knew?

Let me get this straight. When there are bogus, phony, faux, hoax calls to the Coast Guard emergency responders are diverted from real emergencies and situations where people's lives may be at stake. These nitwit brats either don't care about other peoples lives or are so stupid that they cannot comprehend the possible ramifications of their obscene and asinine behavior. 160 bogus calls this year? Three times as many as this time last year? Have they stopped attending raves and need something new to occupy their feeble minds?

No Offense

It's comforting to know that San Francisco's supervisors are constantly thinking of new ways of being politically correct and making sure absolutely no one is offended by anything.

Thanks to new "person first" language guidelines adopted by the board of supervisors a "convicted felon" will now be a "formerly incarcerated person." Parolees will become a "person under supervision" and a juvenile delinquent is now a "young person with justice system involvement." Absolutely hilarious!!!

I'm sure the writers of late night talk show monologs monitor the resolutions of the S.F.B.O.S. on a regular basis for a source of new material. Sanitizing the language used to describe these individuals accomplishes nothing. Parents need to do a better job of instilling the difference between right and wrong in their children and people need to make better behavioral choices. Perhaps then we wouldn't have to spend so much time deciding what to call convicted felons, parolees and juvenile delinquents. Next, I suppose, we will be referring to a murderer as "a person who has sent a fellow human being to a better place."

What Is in a Name?

A SUNK BY ANY OTHER NAME WOULD REEK JUST
as offensively. It would seem there is a lot in a name if you ask the San Francisco
School Board. They recently passed a resolution to rename 44 schools in San
Francisco because those whose names previously adorned those schools have been
deemed unworthy of the honor. Included on the list for purging are such iconic
Americans as George Washington, Thomas Jefferson and Abraham Lincoln.

Thank God Harvey Milk's name was not among the 44 being considered
for reassessment. As any historian can tell you the contributions made by, and
the significance of the career of Harvey Milk trump (pardon the expression) and
far outweigh those made by George Washington, Thomas Jefferson and Abraham Lincoln (combined). After all, Harvey Milk spent four years in the Navy
and rose to the position of San Francisco supervisor. On the other hand George
Washington spent 8 years in the trenches leading the continental Army against
the British in the Revolutionary War and another 8 years as the first President of
the United States. Of course (as you have already noted) we are merely comparing apples and oranges here.

To list the accomplishments of all three of the "purged presidents" would
take several books and if there is one thing we can all agree upon it is that the
world hardly needs another book by yours truly.

One thing that is known for a fact is that none of the three "purged presidents" ever attained the office of supervisor in a city comparable to San Fran-

cisco. This goes a long way in explaining why Harvey Milk has a San Francisco primary school named after him, the Navy has named a ship after him, as well as a high school in New York. You have the Harvey Milk Plaza at Market and Castro streets in the city. The S.F. Gay Democratic Club is now the Harvey Milk Memorial Gay Democratic Club.

In April of 2018 the S.F. Board of Supervisors named terminal 1 at SFO in honor of Harvey Milk. This followed a previous attempt to name the entire airport after him which was turned down. What were they thinking? Not naming the entire airport after Harvey Milk? That is tantamount to not naming the ballpark the Giants play in after Johnnie Lemaster! On May 22, 2014 the USPS issued a stamp honoring Milk as well.

Of course if you can name the most used bridge in the Bay Area (the Willie L. Brown Jr. Bay Bridge) after a crooked politician I guess anything is possible.

I propose a few name changes in the future in order to appease Milk backers who feel his name has not been sufficiently honored. Let's start out with the Harvey Milk Memorial Pentagon. The Harvey Milk Golden Gate Bridge is a no brainer. And Harvey Milk City Hall has a nice ring to it.

It simply shocks and amazes me that no one has suggested the beatification of Saint Harvey the first. Most experts would agree that there is room for one more face on Mr. Rushmore. Can't you imagine the beaming face of Harvey Milk gazing down on us from on high? It gives one goosebumps just thinking about it. Besides if there isn't room for another likeness we just obliterate one or more faces that are taking up space there now. After all the S.F. School Board has declared three of the honorees on Mt. Rushmore to be totally insignificant.

Trans Gender Athletes

It is no wonder that four women from Connecticut filed suit claiming they were forced to play against transgender girls in High school and states are enacting laws that ban transgender athletes from competing in school sports. The Olympic motto "Stronger, higher, faster" sums up perfectly the advantage athletes who were born male would have over their female competitors.

In the 1970's many of us can recall the story of Renée Richards, the former Richard Raskin, competing in women's professional tennis following male to female reassignment surgery. Though Richard Raskind had little or no success against male professional competition the 6'2" Renée Richards rose to number 20 in the women's world rankings in 1979 despite being in her mid-forties. Had Richard Raskind become Renée Richards in her mid-twenties she could have dominated women's tennis for a decade or more.

It doesn't take much imagination to envision transgender females who were born male totally dominating women's sports. If transgender athletes can compete in High school sports why not professional sports or the Olympics? If transgender athletes are allowed to compete in the Olympics there could come a time when virtually all Olympic medals are wond by men or female athletes who were males at birth. Unfair advantages are not what sports are all about.

What a Drag

HEATHER KNIGHT CAN'T BE SERIOUS. WITH SO many issues going on in San Francisco, from getting the Coronavirus vaccine available to as many people as possible to the reopening of our schools so that our children can once again be back in the classroom learning from our teachers, should it really be a priority to keep the Oasis, San Francisco's "Beloved" drag club and cabaret afloat?

After decades of living in the city we have often talked with family members and friends regarding movies we have seen, plays we have attended, concerts we have enjoyed and museums we have visited. Not once has anyone so much as mentioned going to a "Drag Show" to see men dress up as, and pretend to be, women. Nor have they ever expressed a desire to do so.

If we are going to donate money to help perpetuate the arts, as Heather Knight suggests, let's prioritize where it should go. One can learn a lot from attending the cinema, the theater or museums. What exactly is learned from attending a drag queen show? That there are men who are extremely disappointed with the gender God has chosen for them? Is watching men dress up as women, put on wigs, apply makeup and false eyelashes and speak with a falsetto voice to approximate the tone of a female actually entertaining to people? I don't get it. Who finds this pathetic spectacle fun to watch? To me, it's more sad than anything else.

How about contributing to the American Conservatory Theater, Shakespeare in the Park or any other legitimate theater company? Drag shows are just that. A drag.

Recall Chesa Boudin

I AM BEWILDERED BY CHESA BOUDIN apologists who have tried to equate the failed Republican backed campaign to recall Gavin Newsom with the effort to recall Chesa Boudin. These two endeavors have nothing to do with one another.

In addition to Boudin's reluctance to charge violent criminals with the crimes they have committed, resulting in several tragic deaths, we now have Superior Court Judge Bruce Chan quoted as saying "I cannot express in any more certain terms my disapproval of the manner in which the office of the District Attorney is being managed." He goes on to use the words inadvertence and disorganization to describe the culture in the DA's office. He cites constant turnover and managerial reorganization. He describes Boudin's office as overemphasizing criminal justice matters on the "National or state stage" at the expense of "The unglamorous yet necessary work of public prosecution." Deputy public defender Martina Avalos accused prosecutors of routinely failing to turn over potential evidence in a reasonable amount of time and cited three such Brady violations in the past three weeks, calling it a "concerning and recurring pattern." What does any of this have to do with Gavin Newsom? Boudin needs to be removed from the district attorney's office much the same as a malignant tumor needs to be removed from a human body.

Say Goodbye to Chesa Boudin

WITH THE REMOVAL OF CHESA BOUDIN FROM the District Attorney's office it is clear that the pendulum has swung back in the direction of commonsense law enforcement. Under Chesa Boudin too many violent criminals were slapped on the wrist, avoided prosecution and were released back onto the street too often with tragic results. Boudin's tenure was marked by an emphasis on diversion programs that criminals didn't show up for as well as violent perpetrators continuing their lawless agenda while wearing ankle monitors. He is much more concerned with prosecuting police officers than he is with putting career criminals behind bars. In Chesa Boudin's world the phrase "law and order" are anathema. I looked both words up in the dictionary and cannot understand how a city district attorney could find them so distasteful. The results of this recall election has put other "soft on crime" progressive district attorneys on notice. Do the job you were elected to do or face the consequences.

On Chesa Bouin's watch drug dealers who were arrested spent an average of five days in jail. Then they were released from jail so they could continue selling fentanyl to adicts resulting in an overdose epidemic centered in The Tenderloin. Boudin was recalled because time after time he refused to see that violent criminals were charged with the crimes they committed, prosecuted and incarcerated leading to the deaths of innocent victims. People grew tired of Boudin offering (once again) his condolences to the families of people who died because he failed to do his job (think "Groundhog Day"). Who knew violent criminals can continue to commit crimes while wearing an ankle monitor? Not Chesa Boudin. Now he knows.

Having a district attorney who doesn't believe in incarceration is like having a pope who doesn't believe in God and makes as much sense as a pay-toilet in a diarrhea ward.

With mass exodus from the D.A.'s office since Chesa Boudin took over it seems appropriate that Boudin should also exit the premises.

Regarding "Pick Children Over Pets, Pope Tells Couples"

THE COMMENT BY POPE FRANCIS COULD HAVE been aimed directly at San Francisco which has the lowest percentage of children of any city in America. It has been noted that a stroller in the city is more likely to contain a dog than a child.

I have to think, however, that the pope is off base in trying to shame couples into having children when they have no interest in becoming parents. The last thing we need is a lot of selfish, self centered, disinterested parents doing a terrible job of raising children they didn't want in the first place.

Children deserve parents who are totally committed to rearing, nurturing and loving the kids they conceive. We should confine parenting to people who are focused on providing their children with the teaching, mentoring and positive role models their kids need. Those who have decided they would rather provide a home for a dog, a cat or a parakeet should do just that. The world is better off when such people do not have children.

Justin Phillips World of
Black and White

JUSTIN PHILLIPS EXPRESSES DISAPPROVAL OVER
Mayor London Breed's plan to bring more aggressive policing to the Tenderloin
and to "Enforce every single law at our disposal to get (drug users) either into
treatment, or sadly, the alternative is jail." He decries the use of "gun-toting foot
patrols" to help alleviate the problems facing the Tenderloin and offers in its place
"Treatments, education and housing" as a way to cure the epidemic of open drug
dealing and use, overdose fatalities, as well as shootings and stabbings.

The Tenderloin is on life support as a neighborhood and is in a crisis
situation in need of immediate help which London Breed is trying to address.
Something needs to happen now, not in some imagined time in the future when
"Treatment, education and housing" miraculously cure the Tenderloin's myriad
problems. If we wait around for Justin Phillip's hollow platitudes to cure the
problems in the Tenderloin we are in for a long wait.

Other columns by Phillips informed us that Black men make better fathers
than their Caucasian counterparts. Really? Who knew? He also attempted to
discredit the "myth" of the absentee African American father. Since one third of
all Black males between the ages of 18 and 34 are in the criminal justice system,
one can easily imagine how such "myths" get started. It is also (apparently) much

easier to be an exemplary parent while in the criminal justice system than one would logically assume.

He further goes on to explain that the reason 5% of San Francisco's population can account for over 40% of its arrests and incarcerations is simply due to White racism and racial profiling. Yet in the Deep South, where racism and racial profiling is much worse than it is in San Francisco, the percentage of arrests and incarcerations of African Americans isn't anywhere near what it is here. If Mr. Phillips thinks that these amazing statistics can be explained away entirely by "White racism, poverty and a lack of education" he is only fooling himself. There are other factors going on in the Black community that Mr. Phillips chooses to ignore while his head is buried in the sand. Never does Mr. Phillips suggest that any problems besetting Black Americans can be traced to a lack of character, a disregard for the laws of our land, or the willingness to make a living by causing misfortune for innocent victims. Too many African American children are being raised solely by their mother (despite Mr. Phillips' claims) or even their grandmother and grow up hearing the sound of gunfire ringing out in their neighborhoods.

Mr. Phillips sees the world in Black and White. Black is all good. White is all bad. He puts none of the blame on African Americans for any of the negative aspects of the Black experience in American society. They have all been caused by outside influences beyond their control.

Since I first saw a column by Mr. Phillips in the Chronicle I have been waiting to read one that doesn't contain the phrase "People of color." I am still waiting.

Wary of Muslims?

There has been a lot of concern recently about prejudice, bias and animosity that has been directed toward members of the Muslim faith in the Bay Area and indeed the entire nation. Considering the world situation it is not hard to understand why. Your typical human being does not comprehend that every person should be judged as an individual and is not responsible for anyone's actions but their own. They see certain Muslims committing unspeakable crimes against humanity and figure that all Muslims must be of a similar bent.

When virtually every day you open up your newspaper and read about another suicide bombing resulting in the deaths of God knows how many innocent victims and ISIS proudly claims responsibility what are you supposed to think? Often the reason given is the desire by Muslim terrorists to bring about as much death, destruction, mayhem and chaos as possible. Apparently in the Muslim world this makes sense.

In Mali they are content to simply kill Christians indiscriminately. They Have also added kidnapping hundreds of schoolgirls to their repertoire. They endeavor to radicalize them and groom them to be the wives of Islamist terrorists. Whether or not any of these girls ever make it back to their families alive in anyone's guess.

The next days news might include a story about how different sects of the Muslim religion (Sunni and Shiites) are suicide bombing each other in an effort to exterminate those who disagree with their interpretation of the Koran. If these people are not insane then give me another world for it.

When the members of different sects of the same religion decree that members of the other sect do not deserve to live, you are taking religious persecution to a whole new level.

For members of Boko Haram based in Nigeria, suiced bombings and killing civilians at will have become a way of life. Don't forget that portraying an image of the prophet Mohammad warrants a death sentence. A tad harsh (but maybe that's just me). Their goal of ruling the entire world under a single Muslim Caliphate (to me) seems a wee bit extreme. Out of the hundreds of religions that are practiced on our planet it would seem that Islam is the one true religion and all others should be abolished. This kind of arrogant, egotistical and extremist doctrine has led some to surmise that if a religion is to be abolished perhaps it should be the Muslim faith and leave all others to worship in peace. Can you blame them?

How Many Bullets Does It Take to Kill an Unarmed Black Man? (Hint: More Than One Would Logically Assume)

THE POLICE IN AKRON OHIO WERE TAKING NO chances the other day when they pulled Jayland Walker over for "Equipment Violations." Police said Walker fled an attempted traffic stop and fired a shot from his car, yet he was not armed when officers shot him.

Police officers shot Mr. Walker dozens of times with 26 bullets recovered from his body. This raised an obvious question. How many bullets were fired at Mr. Walker that did not penetrate his body? Dozens more perhaps? After all, even the most blood-thirsty sniper (disguised as a police officer) doesn't hit their target every time.

Dr. Lisa Kohler, the Summit County Medical Examiner said it was impossible for her office to say which bullet killed Walker. This poses an obvious problem. If it isn't known which bullet killed Mr. Walker, how will they know who to give the Medal of Valor to for riding the community of an unarmed Black man who posed no threat to anyone? In short, you can't. In this "worst case scenario" no one receives credit for this heroic act of bravery.

The medical examiner's findings confirm that Walker, unarmed and with no drugs or alcohol in his system "Came to a brutal and senseless death." I beg to differ. While the actions of the Akron Police Force can (no doubt) be characterized as brutal I cannot agree that Mr. Walker's death can be described as "senseless." After all, if you riddle a human being with 26 bullets that literally rip his flesh asunder it makes perfect "sense" that it would precipitate his demise.

This incident sheds light on the local motto of the Akron Police Force "The only good Black male is a dead Black male." It would seem to me that the best way to describe this whole travesty is (quite literally) "overkill." We now have word that the Akron Police Department is claiming that Mr. Walker's death was not the result of a massive loss of blood due to 26 gunshot wounds but was brought about by "lead poisoning." Perhaps they have a point.

Afterword

If I have failed to offend anyone by these writings I am truly sorry and I apologize profusely. My intent (as you may have guessed) was to offend every person on Earth (living or dead). If I failed to accomplish my aspiration it was not (I assure you) through a lack of effort. Being offensive has always come naturally to me and I have worked diligently through the years honing my skills. If, however, you read this entire work and were not offended I can only assume you were simply not paying attention. I try to offend indiscriminately without regard to race, color, creed, country of national origin, religious affiliation or marital status. If one possesses the God given talent to offend it should be put to good use and not wasted. I believe I have done just that.

Epilogue

IF THERE IS ONE QUESTION I SIMPLY HAVE TO ask after 70 years on the planet it is can life possibly be as complex, complicated, difficult, hard, confusing, enigmatic and impossible to understand as so many people make it out to be? Listen to a television (or radio) talk show, pick up a newspaper, a magazine, listen to self-help gurus, marriage counselors, politicians, progressives, redneck good old boys, psychiatrists, psychologists, read Dear Abby columns (can some of these letters possibly be real?). Spouses, siblings, friends, parents and children who simply cannot get along and hate each other. Can it really be that hard for us to get along with each other? Divorce courts full of people who married someone they not only didn't love but didn't particularly like (once they got to know them). People getting married two, three, four times or more. "If at first you don't succeed"? After four failed marriages do they still think it's not them, it's the other person?

I would never claim to know the "secret of life" like James Taylor, who tells us in a song of the same name it is to "Enjoy the passage of time." I believe Mr. Taylor is definitely on the right track. I have been listening to James Taylor's music since his self-titled debut album from 1968. A favorite of mine has to be "Carolina in My Mind" (with Paul McCartney on bass). One that resonates with me personally would be "Knockin' Round the Zoo." The song has personal meaning because I have also knocked around a couple of Zoo's myself.

No doubt the highlight of my extended stay was when I was placed in solitary confinement for (so the accusation went) "Insubordination." The sentence that came down was several days of isolation from my fellow incarceratees. Wouldn't want to expose any of them to my evil and devilish influence. In truth I was simply a victim of trumped up charges, hearsay evidence, lies, innuendos, false allegations, misconstrued comments, jealousy, discrimination, hatred, and a desire to simply "rattle my cage." Conspiracy theories were flying about like leaves in a hurricane and chaos was running amok. My personal opinion was that, like Julius Caesar, I had simply become too powerful and influential - and the powers that be chose to place me in complete isolation lest my "Sphere of influence" become too universal. I considered suing but taking legal action is not an option when one is caged like an animal and all rights have been taken away. Somehow I survived (by the skin of my teeth) and lived to tell the tale.

For those who are seeking some kind of meaning or purpose to their life, while I have no desire to preach, I would like to offer a suggestion which may be of some help. I took this bit of advice from a classic pop song popularized by a talented crooner named Perry Como. The song title is "Make Someone Happy" and if it is not the smartest song title ever it is certainly in the top two. Focusing on making someone happy forces you to put your own welfare and concerns on the back burner and to care more about someone else than yourself. As Rupert Holmes put it in his superb pop album "Partners in Crime" you need to "Get outta yourself and get into someone." As the song says, if you do manage to make someone happy, you will be happy too.